Right to Survive

Right to Survive
Human Rights in Nicaragua

Catholic Institute for International Relations

LONDON

First published 1987
Catholic Institute for International Relations
22 Coleman Fields, London N1 7AF

British Library Cataloguing in Publication Data
Right to Survive
Human rights in Nicaragua
    1. Civil rights — Nicaragua
    I. Catholic Institute for International Relations
    323'.4'097285   JC599.N5
    ISBN 0-946848-91-2
    ISBN 0-946848-86-6   Pbk

Design by Jan Brown Designs
Printed in England by the Russell Press Ltd
Bertrand Russell House, Gamble Street, Nottingham NG7 4ET

Contents

Preface

This study attempts to provide an overview of human rights issues in Nicaragua today. It was not undertaken to conduct further research into human rights violations by the government or by the anti-government rebels, the contras. Several reputable organisations such as Amnesty International, Americas Watch, the Inter-American Commission on Human Rights, the International Commission of Jurists and the Washington Office on Latin America have produced regular reports on human rights in Nicaragua. Our concern is not to add detail to these reports but to set out as clearly as possible the issues which they raise and to set them in the context of Nicaragua and Central America today.

Conventionally, a government's human rights record is assessed on the basis of the sum total of human rights violations in a country, which need to be regularly monitored, and this constitutes a government's 'human rights record'. After investigations are completed and reports published, the human rights record, judged good or bad, excellent or appalling, becomes a yardstick by which the outside world is invited to assess the moral legitimacy of a government. Yet judgments based on this material alone may be unjust. The standards set by international human rights declarations and covenants, and the catalogue of violations of them, provide an incomplete evaluation of a government's record, if they are not set in context and historical perspective. At the most obvious level, clearly it is easier to protect human rights in politically stable, economically prosperous countries with a history of developing democratic institutions, than in impoverished nations with a much shorter history of independent statehood and little or no experience of democratic politics, which have yet to develop viable national institutions.

The setting in context of a government's human rights record is doubly important when this record is itself a subject of international controversy. This is the case of Nicaragua where opponents of the Sandinistas, in Nicaragua and elsewhere, seek to portray the government as a gross violator of human rights. Because of the enormous importance which judgments about Nicaragua's human rights record assume in such circumstances, it is essential not only that the evidence on which they are based be trustworthy but that the judgments themselves be fair. The question of fairness involves, apart from careful examination of the evidence, looking at the factors which help or obstruct the effective protection of human rights. In other words, if judgment is to be fair, the political, social and economic context in which human rights are upheld or violated must also be examined. This study attempts to provide that context: regional, historical and contemporary.

Acknowledgements

CIIR wishes to thank SIDA (Swedish International Development Authority) for the generous grant which enabled us to publish this book. We must thank also the many people in Nicaragua, of all shades of opinion, who spoke freely and passionately about human rights, and those who took the trouble to read and comment on early manuscripts. If they read the book as published, they will find that much of their criticism is reflected in the text.

Abbreviations

ANPDH — *Asociación Nicaragüense Pro Derechos Humanos,* group linked to armed opposition to monitor human rights abuses by contra forces.

AHPROCAFE — *Asociación Hondureña de Productores de Café,* Association of Honduran Coffee Producers.

ARDE — *Alianza Revolucionaria Democrática,* contra group based in Costa Rica, now dissolved, led by Edén Pastora and Alfonso Robelo.

ATC — *Asociación de Trabajadores del Campo,* Sandinista rural labourers' union.

CAUS — *Central de Acción y Unidad Sindical,* trade union confederation affiliated to the Nicaraguan Communist Party.

CEPAD — *Comité Evangélico Pro-Ayuda al Desarrollo,* organisation of Protestant churches, mainly evangelical and pentecostal, carrying out development and education work. Founded in 1973 after the Managua earthquake of 23 December 1972.

CIDCA — *Centro de Investigación de la Costa Atlántica,* Nicaraguan government research and study centre dealing with the Atlantic Coast.

CGTI — *Central General de Trabajadores Independiente,* trade confederation affiliated to the Socialist Party.

CNPPDH — *Comisión Nacional por la Protección y Promoción de los Derechos Humanos,* human rights commission funded by the Nicaraguan government.

CODEH — *Comisión de Derechos Humanos de Honduras,* independent commission monitoring human rights in Honduras.

COSEP — *Consejo Superior de la Empresa Privada*, Superior Council of Private Enterprise, grouping of major private businesses in Nicaragua, strongly anti-government, a member of the opposition coalition *Coordinadora Democrátic Nicaragüense.*

CPDH — *Comisión Permanente de los Derechos Humanos*, independent human rights commission critical of Nicaraguan government.

CST — *Central Sandinista de Trabajo*, Sandinista trade union confederation.

CTN — *Central de Trabajadores de Nicaragua*, trade union confederation aligned with Social Christian Party.

CUS — *Consejo de Unificación Sindical*, trade union confederation aligned with Social Democrat Party.

DGSE — *Dirección General de Seguridad del Estado*, Directorate General of State Security, Nicaraguan security police attached to the Ministry of the Interior.

ECLA — Economic Commission for Latin America, an agency of the UN.

EPS — *Ejército Popular Sandinista*, Nicaraguan Army.

FAO — *Frente Amplio Opositora*, Broad Opposition Front, political grouping opposed to Somoza which sought a negotiated rather than an unconditional end to the dictatorship.

FETSALUD — *Federación de Trabajadores de la Salud*, health service union.

FDN — *Fuerzas Democráticas Nicaragüenses*, major contra group operating from Honduras.

FRS — *Fuerzas Revolucionarias Sandinistas*, contra group led by Edén Pastora, part of the ARDE coalition.

FSLN — *Frente Sandinista de Liberación Nacional*, Sandinista Front for National Liberation.

IACHR — Interamerican Commission on Human Rights, part of the Organisation of American States.

ICRC — International Committee of the Red Cross.

ILO — International Labour Office.

JGRN — *Junta de Gobierno de Reconstrucción Nacional*, ruling government council between 1979 and 1984.

MISURASATA — *Miskito, Sumu, Rama, Sandinista Aslatakanka*, indigenous organisation on the Atlantic Coast which at first worked with government. Subsequently adopted as name of mainly Miskito contra organisation.

PCDN — *Partido Conservador Democrático*, Democratic

	Conservative Party, ran in elections, winning 14 seats.
PLI	— *Partido Liberal Independiente,* Independent Liberal Party, ran in elections, winning 9 seats in the National Assembly.
PPSC	— *Partido Popular Social Cristiano,* Popular Social Christian Party, ran in elections, winning 6 seats.
PSC	— *Partido Social Cristiano,* Social Christian Party, boycotted elections.
PSD	— *Partido Social Demócrata,* Social Democratic Party, boycotted elections.
TPA	— *Tribunal Popular Antisomocista,* special court for trying security-related offences.
UCA	— *Universidad Centroamericana,* Catholic University in Managua.
UDEL	— *Unión Democrática de Liberación,* Democratic Liberation Union, anti-Somoza coalition led by Pedro Joaquín Chamorro in the 1970s.
UNHCR	— United Nations High Commissioner for Refugees.
UNO	— *Unión Nacional Opositora,* National Opposition Union, contra coordinating body.
UNO-CDH	— *Unión Nacional Opositora — Comisión de Derechos Humanos,* UNO Human Rights Commission.

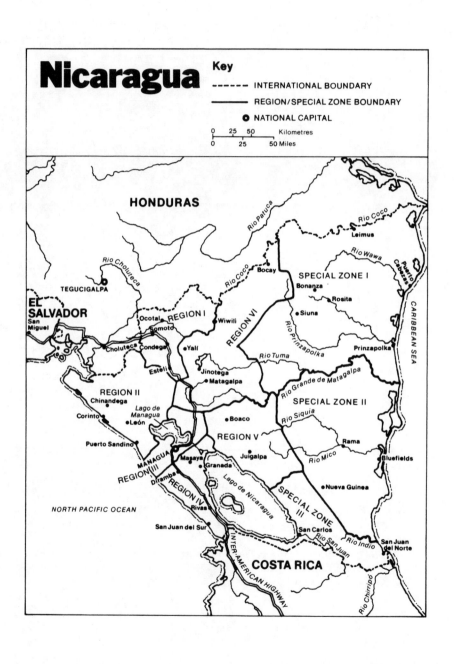

Nicaragua

Key

------ INTERNATIONAL BOUNDARY

—— REGION/SPECIAL ZONE BOUNDARY

◉ NATIONAL CAPITAL

```
0    25   50      Kilometres
0    25      50 Miles
```

HONDURAS

Rio Patuca

Rio Coco

Leimus

Rio Wawa

Rio Choluteca

Bocay

SPECIAL ZONE I

Puerto Cabezas

TEGUCIGALPA

Rio Coco

Bonanza

Rosita

EL SALVADOR

San Miguel

Ocotal

REGION I

Wiwili

REGION VI

Siuna

CARIBBEAN SEA

Somoto

Rio Prinzapolka

Choluteca

Condega

Yalí

Rio Tuma

Prinzapolka

Estelí

Jinotega

Matagalpa

REGION II

Chinandega

Rio Grande de Matagalpa

SPECIAL ZONE II

Corinto

Lago de Managua

León

Boaco

Rio Siquia

SPECIAL ZONE II

Rama

Puerto Sandino

REGION V

Rio Mico

Bluefields

MANAGUA

REGION III

Masaya

Granada

Juigalpa

SPECIAL ZONE III

Diramba

REGION IV

Lago de Nicaragua

Nueva Guinea

NORTH PACIFIC OCEAN

Rivas

San Carlos

Rio Indio

San Juan del Norte

San Juan del Sur

Rio San Juan

INTER-AMERICAN HIGHWAY

COSTA RICA

Rio Chirripó

1. Introduction

1. Basic human rights

The Universal Declaration of Human Rights, with its 30 articles, sets standards by which human rights in a given country can be assessed. Approved by 48 states at the United Nations in 1948, the Universal Declaration of Human Rights represents the aspirations and ideals of the democratic powers and their allies after World War II. Some of the most fundamental rights it contains are hard-won achievements written into law over several centuries in Western Europe and North America. As one human rights lawyer has put it:

> The various laws, declarations, bills and covenants on human rights sound so principled and majestic that they are often taken as just a product of a happy blend of statesmanship and scholarship. Yet, in reality, the driving force behind these documents has invariably been the struggle of people demanding recognition and respect for their rights. This essential feature in the history of human rights is not always sufficiently stressed.[1]

The rights contained in the Universal Declaration of Human Rights fall easily into two categories: civil and political rights, set out in Articles 3 to 21, and economic and social rights in Articles 22 to 27. The reports of human rights groups concentrate on the violation of those human rights clearly established in international law, leaving out, or attaching less importance to, economic and social rights. Human rights groups are Western, in ideology if not always in location, and Western-style democracies have never taken economic and social rights as seriously as political and civil rights. Furthermore, economic and social rights constitute an area in which the obligations of governments to their citizens are less clearly defined and in which it is more difficult to make an objective assessment of a government's performance. To ordinary people, however, both sorts of rights are of fundamental importance. Certainly gross violations of either are experienced as equally calamitous in human and personal terms.

For the purposes of this study, we propose another division, into basic human rights and subsidiary rights. The human rights we classify as basic are those without which the remaining human rights cannot be enjoyed, that is, those guaranteeing life, physical integrity (freedom from torture), freedom from arbitrary detention and adequate access to all that is necessary to sustain life. Thus some civil and political rights and one economic right are treated as basic. The first part of Article 25 states: 'Everyone has the right to a standard of living adequate for the health and well-being of himself and his family, including food, clothing, and medical care and necessary social services . . .' In other words, basic human needs are treated as human rights. It is not claimed that subsidiary human rights are unimportant, simply that basic human rights are logically and morally prior to the rest. Without the fulfilment of basic needs and the protection of life and personal security, the others cannot be enjoyed.

Basic human rights are inherent in the human person in any situation. In society human rights are claimed by the bearers of those rights against someone or something which has the obligation and the ability to grant them, and are guaranteed by law or are susceptible to guarantee by law. In the modern world civil and political rights are claimed against the state, which in its turn has the obligation to guarantee them. For that reason, human rights violations, by definition committed by the state, are viewed as particularly grave offences.

Subsidiary rights include the right to take part in and choose the government of one's country by genuine elections; freedom of expression and opinion; the right of peaceful assembly; freedom of movement; the right to a free choice of employment and to equality in employment; the right to participate in the cultural life of the community. All these, and other subsidiary rights, are significant components of the quality of life, but they are not basic rights.

Basic needs as basic rights
How do basic needs make their appearance as basic human rights?[2] Can they also be claimed as a right by an individual against the state? Is failure by the state to attend to such basic needs a human rights violation? In *moral* terms, a strong argument can be made that malnutrition, high rates of infant mortality, the prevalence of easily preventable diseases, hunger and ignorance do constitute gross violations of human rights, particularly in those countries where the

availability of resources is such that these social ills could be cured by a change in economic priorities. In *legal* terms and in practice, however, the answer is no. This is reflected in the International Covenant on Economic, Social and Cultural Rights, which uses only the language of intention to express states' obligations:

> Each State Party to the present Covenant undertakes to take steps . . . to the maximum of its available resources . . . with a view to achieving progressively the full realisation of the rights recognised in the present Covenant by all appropriate means, including particularly the adoption of legislative measures [Article 2].

Basic human needs, nonetheless, have entered the language of human rights and international human rights organisations, such as the International Commission of Jurists and the Inter-American Commission on Human Rights (IACHR), which include sections on governments' economic and social policies as part of their reports on human rights. The IACHR, for instance, has stated:

> The essence of the legal obligation incurred by any government in this area is to strive to attain the economic and social aspirations of its people, by following an order that assigns priority to the basic needs of health, nutrition and education. The priority of 'rights of survival' and 'basic needs' is a natural consequence of the right to personal security.[3]

The denial of basic economic and social needs becomes an issue of basic human rights particularly when it affects large numbers of people and, above all, when it it is a structural condition of life for the majority of the population, that is, a situation which is maintained by the policies of a minority ruling elite. This, with the exception of present-day Nicaragua and Costa Rica, is the case in Central America where the generalised violation of basic economic and social rights is well nigh universal. While poor, the countries of Central America are not among the poorest in the world. The gross deprivation of the majority of the population, that is, the denial of these basic human rights, is not so much the consequence of a lack of resources with which to satisfy them as of political, economic and social structures which perpetuate their denial by concentrating wealth and income in the hands of a small minority. In theory, a government's record in this area is the product of its will and ability to change those structures in order to achieve the full realisation of those rights. In fact, it is determined by the balance of power between the sectional interests which it represents and which frequently exercise direct control over the state as well as the government and its policies. At the same time, it is recognised that natural disasters, the weather and international markets constitute external factors over which the government of a developing country has no control. Social and economic structures, however, such as the pattern of land ownership and land use and the power of the military or a particular social class, are precisely the obstacles to development which should be addressed by a government, by legislative measures, as enjoined by the Covenant.

In the case of the Somoza government in Nicaragua, there was manifestly no intention of taking any such measures. On the contrary, the economic record of the dictatorship is one of continual exertion to deny those rights. The appropriation by Somoza and his circle of the international aid which flowed into the country after the earthquake of 23 December 1972 demonstrated that he and his government were openly contemptuous of the most urgent humanitarian needs of ordinary Nicaraguans. In an older language, Somoza did not govern in the interests of the common good. He was a tyrant.

Civil and political rights

Basic civil and political rights are as significant as basic economic and social rights. International covenants, however, are much more specific about states' obligations to their citizens in this area. The International Covenant on Civil and Political Rights stipulates that the rights to life and not to be subjected to torture, among others, are unconditional. It is not necessary to establish at length that these rights are indeed basic human rights.

Economic and social rights are concerned with the condition of the majority. Civil and political rights, while defining liberties and rights which should be enjoyed by the whole population, enshrine guarantees that are of particular concern to minorities and individuals, and are, by their nature, tested by opposition groups, dissidents, critics and non-conformists. These rights, if effective, enable citizens to organise politically in order to bring about changes in the composition and policies of their governments and, in competitive electoral systems, to put their parties forward as alternative governments. They include the freedoms of association, speech and religion, the right to a fair trial, to freedom from arbitrary detention, and to take part in the government of the country either directly or through chosen representatives.

In Central America these rights too have been systematically violated. Indeed, the violation of these rights is closely related to the violation of basic economic and social rights. The struggle of the poor to obtain recognition of their civil and political rights has gone hand in hand with their struggle for economic conditions to ensure an adequate standard of living. In Nicaragua under Somoza, El Salvador and Guatemala, the consistent denial of all these rights blocked all possibilities of peaceful change and led directly to armed rebellion.

2. States of emergency and legitimacy

Civil and political rights, however, are precisely those rights which may be restricted at a time of national emergency. There are few exceptions. Article 27 of the American Convention on Human Rights, which Nicaragua ratified and incorporated into law in 1979, states:

> In time of war, public danger, or other emergency that threatens the independence or security of a State Party, it may take measures derogating from its obligations under the present Convention to the extent and for the period of time strictly required by the exigencies of the situation . . .

The following rights may not be suspended: the right to juridical personality, the right to life, the right to humane treatment, freedom from slavery, freedom from *ex post facto* laws, freedom of conscience and religion, the rights of the family, the right to a name, the right of the child, the right to nationality and the right to participate in government. The right not to be arbitrarily detained and the right to a fair trial, however, are among those rights which may be suspended.

There are examples in the recent history of many governments, democratic or otherwise, of restrictions being imposed on civil and political rights in the face of an external or internal threat. States of emergency are habitually used by dictatorships when faced with internal dissent and are a demonstration of their lack of popular support. In general, criticism of such measures focuses on the legitimacy of the government taking the measures, the reality of the threat which it is facing, and the question of whether the measures taken are proportional to the threat which they are intended to contain or avert.

Because a state of emergency suspends some important human rights, the only valid argument that can be made for the declaration of a state of emergency is that it is being made to ensure the survival of society and therefore defend human rights. This has to be demonstrated in practice. The case of the government declaring the state of emergency is enormously strengthened if it can demonstrate that it owes its legitimacy to properly conducted and genuine elections. This is the case with Nicaragua today.

Fulfilling a promise made before the insurrection, in February 1984 the provisional government (*Junta de Gobierno de Reconstrucción Nacional*

— JGRN) called for general elections in November for a president and for a National Assembly which was also to act as a constituent assembly, drawing up and approving the new constitution. These elections were observed by many foreign delegations, some of them expert election watchers, and were generally recognised as fair. The election observers regretted that the parties that made up the *Coordinadora Democrática*, with Arturo Cruz as their designated candidate, did not participate but they did not change their view of the election. There was an 80% turn-out. The Sandinistas won 66 per cent of the valid votes cast and 66 seats in the 100-member National Assembly. The Nicaraguan Conservative Party won 14 seats, the Independent Liberal Party 9 and the Popular Social Christian Party 6. Daniel Ortega, who had been the Coordinator of the JGRN and *de facto* head of state, was elected President for a six-year term. The elections show that the FSLN now heads a government demonstrably based on popular consent and can reasonably expect to receive the recognition routinely afforded to elected governments anywhere in the world.

The nature of the threat to the security and independence of Nicaragua and the scope of the state of emergency are discussed later in the text.

3. Context and balance

Human rights organisations almost never compare the record of one government with that of another lest they be accused of special pleading, seeking to explain away or justify one abuse by reference to another. Their findings, however, are available to others who may wish to make such comparisons. In the case of Nicaragua, the most telling comparisons are to be found in the recent history of Western democratic nations and are never mentioned in reports on Nicaragua. This fact alone causes Nicaraguans to react to these reports more as sanctimonious condemnation than constructive criticism and to read them for their political impact on solidarity and support rather than out of concern for human rights.

The starting point for the Nicaraguan government is that Nicaragua is a country at war, under attack by forces which, in all but the nationality of their troops, are the forces of a foreign power. The Nicaraguans, however, are aware of the human rights records of the countries where Nicaragua's human rights record is debated and especially of the way in which human rights have been violated or restricted during war-time. The most commonly mentioned examples of the abuse or restriction by Western democracies of human rights during war-time are the deportation by the US government of more than 100,000 Japanese Americans from California to internment camps in Arizona during the Second World War, the use of internment and the modification of trial procedures (the Diplock courts) by the British government in Northern Ireland during the 1970s and 1980s, and the use of censorship in both the UK and the US to stifle criticism during the Second World War.

The behaviour of civil police forces in Western countries today and cases of arbitrary and sometimes brutal treatment of minorities and protesters rarely enter into the discussion of human rights. Abuses committed by police forces are commonplace and are not limited to situations of war or emergency. One measure of a nation's commitment to human rights is the practical steps which its government takes to help citizens obtain redress against police abuses and its willingness to prosecute and impose appropriate punishment on police officers found guilty of abuses.

This report concentrates on the human rights record of the Nicaraguan government. It does so because the government is responsible for protecting and upholding human rights and civil liberties throughout Nicaragua. Less space is devoted to contra atrocities. One possible consequence of this imbalance between accounts of the government's and the contras' behaviour might be the impression that contra atrocities are equated with or even regarded as less important than, say, the government's restrictions on the freedom of expression under the state of emergency. This is not the case. Examples of a few contra atrocities are described and discussed in detail. It should be remembered that they are examples, standing for hundreds of similar deliberate murders, indiscriminate attacks on civilians, and cases of torture, rape, mutilation and kidnapping.

Such atrocities neither excuse nor justify violations of human rights by the Nicaraguan government. Nor would the restrictions on civil liberties in force in Nicaragua necessarily be different if the contras were a disciplined military force not given to the murder and kidnapping of civilians. Nevertheless the contra atrocities are a crucial element in the debate on human rights in Nicaragua because they are often compared with abuses committed by the government and because the Reagan administration and its allies have sought repeatedly to misrepresent the situation in Nicaragua, overlooking violations committed by the contras and exaggerating or inventing abuses committed by the government.

4. The new state

It is now over seven years since the victory of 19 July 1979 which removed General Somoza from power and placed the Sandinista Front for National Liberation (FSLN) at the head of a provisional revolutionary government. Since then, the Nicaraguans have been engaged in three major tasks — the consolidation of new political institutions, development and defence.

The Nicaraguans have never had any experience of democracy in their own country. For 45 years up to July 1979 Nicaragua was governed by the Somozas, a family dictatorship which, by the time it was overthrown, was a political anachronism even in Central American terms. Shortly before Anastasio Somoza, the first of the line, made himself president, Nicaragua lived through a period of civil war and occupation by US troops. For 16 years before this US intervention, Nicaragua had been governed by the nationalist autocrat José Santos Zelaya.

The Somozas did little to assist the development of a modern state. They ran Nicaragua like a feudal estate. Power and privilege depended on the personal patronage of the president. The National Guard, combining the functions of police and army, was first and foremost a private army. The Somozas bribed, manipulated and intimidated the opposition; they used their political power to gain control of businesses and land, and what they were not interested in they simply neglected. There were families and business groups, independent of the Somozas or even in opposition to them, which prospered during the years of economic growth, but their considerable economic power was not, as is customary in capitalist countries, reflected in political power. As individuals they were always vulnerable to intimidation or blandishments from the dynasty. Taking their example from and being the creatures of their heads of state, the judges, the National Guard and the civil service were hopelessly corrupt. In 1979 there was little that was worth preserving from the old regime. In 1979, therefore, the FSLN and its allies not only had the immediate tasks of reconstruction before them but also had to lay the foundations of a new state, including those institutions — the judiciary, a representative elected legislature, police force, army, security forces — which are charged with the impartial protection of all citizens and the protection and promotion of human rights. The majority of those who took on these tasks were untrained. Many of the faults found with the behaviour of the army and the security forces today can be traced to this lack of education and training for tasks which are by definition difficult and sensitive.

The fact that the government of Nicaragua derives its legitimacy, in formal terms, from the convincing victory of the FSLN in elections generally recognised as honest and fair does not exhaust the issue of legitimacy. Such a new state also faces the wider and more difficult problem of securing national consensus around itself, its institutions and constitutional priorities. Clearly popular support for the state and its institutions needs to be wider than the support demonstrated for any one party in elections, even the majority party, because it is these institutions which decide who will govern, allocate scarce resources and determine national priorities. In other words, the state needs the support and loyalty of those who lose in elections or feel that their interests are in some way harmed by the political party in power. The difficulties of creating such a consensus around new institutions in the aftermath of a revolution can readily be appreciated. In Nicaragua, as we have pointed out, such difficulties were exacerbated by the feudal character of the Somozas and the lack of a national experience of democratic politics. In mature democratic societies such support and loyalty are manifested in the compliance by specific groups or entire sections of the population with policies prejudicial to their interests because they accept the government of the day as legitimate. In such societies the genuine and spontaneous patriotism demonstrated in times of national crisis is typically the product of many years of development of democratic institutions which are seen as responsive, or potentially responsive, to popular, majority demands.

The possibility of securing the support and loyalty of political opponents of the new state will be enhanced if new institutions are established which provide effective protection for human rights and a mechanism for peaceful changes of government, that is, periodic and free elections.

It cannot be taken for granted that, had Nicaragua been left in peace to develop along its own lines after the revolution, it would have progressed smoothly towards a new national consensus. The resignations of Alfonso Robelo and Arturo Cruz,[4] and other high-ranking government officials, and their subsequent enrolment in the contra cause, show that there was greater agreement about the need to overthrow the Somoza dictatorship than about the sort of state institutions which should replace it. Nonetheless the conduct and result of the elections held in 1984 suggest that a national consensus about the new state and its priorities was not beyond possibility. They were held despite threats of disruption by the contras and a boycott led by the *Coordinadora Nacional Democrática*. The result demonstrated the enormous popularity of the FSLN. In the face of the obvious advantages enjoyed by the FSLN, the performance of the divided and poorly organised opposition parties, which won 33 per cent of the valid votes, is evidence of the relative openness of the elections. The destabilisation of Nicaragua through the contra war is intended precisely to destroy the emerging national consensus demonstrated in the elections and subsequently in the debate on the constitution.

5. The war

The war against the contras and its effect on the economy have come to dominate all other issues in Nicaragua. What started as erratic and isolated attacks by former members of Somoza's defeated National Guard, and was no more than an irritant to the new government, has become an organised campaign to destabilise and overthrow the Sandinista government, a campaign which is sponsored, financed and directed by the US government. The war affects every area of life in Nicaragua. The diversion of resources into defence from other areas of the economy has become a haemorrhage which not only holds back current development programmes but is also undermining and destroying what was achieved in the early years of the revolution, and is now threatening the economic fabric of the country.

The war is a crushing extra burden imposed on a poor country which did not have time to recover from the effects of the war of insurrection against the Somoza dictatorship. In 1977, the last year of 'normal' economic activity before the revolution, GDP per head was US $1,265 a year (1980 value). Now it is estimated at $710 a year.[5]

The war is a total war. As one of its theorists has stated, low intensity conflict is 'total war at the grass roots level', in which the military element comes fourth in order of importance, behind the political, economic and social components.[6] The war is intended by the US government to provoke economic crisis, fostering widespread discontent and encouraging the creation of internal political movements which will undermine the Sandinista government's ability to mobilise the country for defence and prepare the ground for possible external intervention. It is certainly not intended to create an environment propitious for human rights.

The implications for human rights are complex. The war has many of the characteristics of an international conflict. It is financed, sponsored and directed by a foreign power, the United States. There can be little doubt that, without the support of the United States government, the contras today would be much less of a threat, if they existed at all. The war provides a *prima facie* justification for many of the restrictions placed on civil and political rights. A judgment needs to be made as to whether, in the light of the threat posed by the contra war, the measures contained in the states of emergency which have been in force in Nicaragua for all but 16 months since 19 July 1979 are 'reasonable'.

6. Human rights since 1979

One month after taking power, on 21 August 1979, the new

government issued Decree No. 52, the Statute of the Rights and Guarantees of Nicaraguans, restating the rights of the Universal Declaration of Human Rights and adding some more. The statute abolishes the death penalty in Nicaragua. It also makes clear that in times of emergency all but the most basic rights may be suspended. The following year the government ratified the American Convention on Human Rights (25 September 1979) and the International Covenant on Human Rights (12 March 1980), together with the optional protocol to the covenant on Civil and Political Rights. In April 1985 Nicaragua signed the United Nations Convention against Torture and other Cruel, Inhuman or Degrading Treatment or Punishment.[7]

This study does not examine Nicaragua's record on each and every right set out in these treaties and in the Statute of Rights and Guarantees. Particular importance is given to basic human rights, including those economic rights which have been included in this category, and there is a detailed examination of trial procedures. Civil and political rights are dealt with under the heading of the freedoms of expression, association and religion. An attempt has been made to quantify human rights violations. Even though the precise accuracy of such figures cannot be guaranteed, they are indicative of the state of human rights, particularly in the cases of the most serious violations, such as extra-judicial executions. The cases on which the most serious accusations against the government are based have been described here so that readers may judge for themselves.

7. The politics of 'human rights'.

The discussion of human rights in Nicaragua today is a political argument. Different versions of the government's human rights record have been used to influence international opinion. The Reagan administration, with scant regard for the truth, has made a concerted effort to paint as evil a picture as possible of Nicaragua, describing it as a 'totalitarian dungeon'. Supporters of the Sandinistas have produced lengthy critiques of the Amnesty International and Americas Watch reports. They have argued that Nicaragua has a good record of human rights compared to other Central American countries and have compared Nicaragua with examples of other countries at war.[8]

Enmeshed in this argument is the question of the 'real' intentions of the Sandinistas. The contras and the Reagan administration want the world to see the Nicaraguan government as totalitarian. They maintain that if the FSLN is allowed to establish itself firmly in power then internal opposition will be extinguished and that such openness as has been permitted will be revealed as a sham used only to deceive public opinion. They base their argument on the fact that the majority of the Sandinista leadership are Marxists or Marxist-Leninists, as their pre-revolutionary writings show, and that they are now receiving the military support of the Soviet bloc. Such arguments deliberately overlook the record of the past eight years.

The Sandinista government has been qualitatively different from any other left-wing revolutionary government — particularly the Cuban revolutionary government which overthrew General Batista in 1959. The nationalist and Christian strands in 'sandinismo' have been as influential as the marxist components. The abolition of the death penalty, the humane penal system, the passing of a generous amnesty law for those who have taken up arms against the government and the willingness to reach agreements with political opponents are not hallmarks of governments normally labelled as totalitarian.

This argument is relevant to human rights. It is clear that the Sandinistas do see themselves as a revolutionary vanguard. In their view, this gives them a moral authority which opponents, however honourable, do not have. This leads them to treat opponents in different ways. They are prepared to be merciful towards captured contras despite their record of terrorism, rehabilitating them in a relatively humane prison system. They are tolerant of the traditional opposition parties which participate in the National Assembly. The Sandinistas, however, have difficulty in dealing with determined opponents with a sharply opposed ideology, particularly those who, while denying any connection with the contras, profess a Christian identity as the political antithesis of everything the Sandinistas stand for. However unclear the views of such people might be in concrete political terms, it is evident that they are uncompromising opponents of the Sandinistas and aspire to a very different sort of society from that which the Sandinistas are seeking to build in Nicaragua. Although they have not taken up arms or openly advocated taking up arms, some of these opponents have been described by government officials as 'ideological contras'. A few have been detained, threatened and interrogated by the DGSE, the security police, about alleged links with the contras, spending, in the worst cases, several weeks in detention.

This sector of the opposition explicitly rejects the constitutional framework and structures which are slowly being built up to regulate political competition. It would be difficult enough in peace-time to accommodate such sharply opposing views and their corresponding political parties in a competitive electoral system created from scratch after a revolution. The war is an added complication, for it is these opponents who enjoy the support of the leading Catholic bishops and who are used by the US government to justify its support of the contras to the US public and world opinion.

The war, this 'total war at the grass-roots level', thus clouds human rights issues. Because of the war the international community has not been able to assess how the Sandinistas and the internal opposition would have fared in the task of creating and consolidating new institutions in peace-time, nor how the Sandinistas would have attempted to cope with the contradictions of being a vanguard party pledged to political pluralism.

The war which is being waged against Nicaragua by the most powerful nation on earth requires a national response. In such a war a simple majority is not enough. What the Nicaraguan government needs for successful survival and resistance is the overwhelming support of the population. The war is clearly intended by its strategists to drive a wedge between the Sandinistas and the rest of the population and to undermine the capacity of the government to mobilise for defence. The human rights violations which the government has committed in the course of the war stem from this situation. The government is least tolerant of those who, without being contras, do not accept the war as a national war for the common good and resent the sacrifices which it imposes, agreeing with the Catholic bishops, who in 1983 described the conscription law introduced by the government as military conscription at the service of an ideology.

The greatest violator of human rights in Nicaragua is neither the Sandinistas nor the contras but the US government. In order to make the Sandinistas 'say uncle',[9] in order to re-establish unchallenged US control over a region which it regards as its backyard, the US government has sacrificed over 20,000 Nicaraguan lives, most of them contras, and caused untold suffering. The objectives of the war are framed in terms of US interests and in the rhetoric of democracy and freedom. For the Nicaraguans, though, it is a different story. The contras are improbable standard-bearers of tolerance and democratic values. Even the most detached assessments predict that a contra victory would usher in a period of prolonged bloodshed and instability. In terms of the human rights which the US government professes to champion, the 'cure' would be, and already is, many times worse than the disease.

The ultimate consequences of the contra war have yet to be experienced. It remains to be seen whether it has destroyed or simply postponed any possibility of the creation of a new national consensus around a new state, seen and experienced as legitimate by the great majority of Nicaraguans. Only such a consensus will permit the creation of viable legal and social institutions in which the protection of human rights can flourish. The destruction of this consensus was clearly the intention of those who planned the contra war from the beginning.

2. The Central American Context

This chapter outlines the major economic and social problems of Central America as they have developed over the past 40 years and charts the deterioration in the living standards of the majority of the population. These problems are common to the whole region. Political forces, structures and responses differ. The FSLN's revolutionary response is placed in the context of a region where, with the exception of Costa Rica, violence has been the most common response of governments to the demand for social change. In the 1970s, reformist political movements won popular support in Guatemala and El Salvador. The dismal record of repression, which put an end to their hopes of peaceful change, provides some justification for the FSLN's contention that it is only through a revolution that significant change can be accomplished. Today Nicaragua has the only government in Central America that can make the basic needs of the majority its highest social and economic priority.

1. Economic and social development in Central America

The Nicaraguan insurrection was one of three major guerrilla upheavals at the end of the 1970s. At the time of the Sandinista victory El Salvador and Guatemala were already moving towards large-scale guerrilla wars. These conflicts have common roots in extreme poverty and the intransigence of ruling classes unwilling to concede even the slightest economic and social reforms to defuse political tension. These purely domestic processes have been distorted by long-standing US interest in the region and, most recently, by the contra war against Nicaragua now openly sponsored by the Reagan administration. For the ordinary people of Central America, the consequence has been a decade of social upheaval, marked by extreme economic difficulty and widespread and systematic human rights violations.

Between 1950 and 1980 there was rapid economic and population growth in Central America. The population grew from 8 million to 20 million. Between 1950 and 1978 the GDP of the region as a whole grew by 5.3% a year, with the highest rates in Nicaragua and Costa Rica and the lowest in Honduras.[1] In *per capita* terms, this was growth from annual income of US$242 (1950) to $428 (1978) at 1979 prices.[2] This economic growth was the result of agricultural diversification, the development of sugar and cotton as export crops and the raising of livestock to supplement foreign earnings from coffee. One of the effects of the introduction of these new plantation crops was the displacement of peasants from their lowland holdings, aggravating the problem of landlessness. The creation of the Central American Common Market in 1960 boosted the economies of the region for about ten years, but its possibilities of growth were restricted by social structures which concentrated purchasing power in a tiny elite and a small middle class. Economic growth bypassed the poor or made them worse off.

> While it (economic growth) vastly increased the wealth of a few and modestly enhanced the income of a considerably larger number, its net effect on the poorer classes — 60 to 80 per cent of the population in Guatemala, Nicaragua, Honduras and El Salvador — varied from marginal enhancement to absolute deprivation. Rapid growth meant inflation, which is disastrous for those without the means and leverage to keep ahead of price increases. And rapid growth encouraged the rationalisation of agricultural enterprise through the substitution of machinery and wage labour for tenant farmers. When the appetite for profit maximisation penetrates less developed areas it leads also to extra-legal land seizures by officers and oligarchs in control of the state machinery.[3]

In Guatemala, between 1950 and 1964, the number of farms under one hectare in area, sub-subsistence plots much smaller than the minimum needed to sustain a peasant family, increased from 74,259 to 85,083. Over the same period the area of land per rural inhabitant went down from 1.3 to 0.8 hectares.[4] As economic growth continued through the 1960s and 1970s, the situation of the poor deteriorated. Between 1960 and 1974 the performance of Guatemalan export agriculture outstripped that of all but two other Latin American countries. Domestic food production lagged behind. The area occupied by peasant farms shrank by 26% during the 1970s while the area devoted to export crops increased by 45%. Seasonal migrants, who live on tiny plots in the Guatemalan highlands, travelling every year to the plantations, became 49% of the total rural labour force.[5] In 1970 a US Agency for International Development team concluded, 'Guatemala's economic and social development record has been poor. There is little doubt that the absolute standard of living of a large part of the population has declined.'[6] At the same time Guatemala's tiny agricultural and business elite grew richer: in 1950 the top 5% of the population received 48% of the national income; by 1978 their share had grown to 59%.

The experience in El Salvador was similar. The area of land held in peasant-owned plots of less than one hectare was 56% greater in 1961 than in 1950, and there were corresponding decreases in the total area held in family-sized farms of 5-10 and 10-20 hectares, the result of population growth and the expulsion of the rural population from new plantation lands.[7] This process continued in the following decade: between 1961 and 1971 the number of plots of less than one hectare increased from 70,400 to 132,900.[8] The proportion of the rural population without land increased from 12% in 1961 to 29% in 1971 and 41% in 1975. At the other end of the scale there was a corresponding concentration of wealth and income: by 1966, 3,000 families controlled 43% of all cultivated land, 33% of the national territory. 463 properties accounted for 29% of cultivated land and 23% of the national territory.[9] The rapid growth of industry during the 1960s and early 1970s was no solution to this extreme social and economic polarisation: manufacturing output expanded by 24% but jobs in manufacturing went up by only 6%. These grim statistics were reflected in the quality of life of the Salvadorean people. In the 1970s, 8% of the population received 50% of the national income, with the remaining 92% sharing the other half.[10] El Salvador's record in the provision of health care, nutrition and literacy, and its infant mortality figures, are among the worst in Latin America.

Honduras, while the poorest country of Central America, escaped the social tension caused by the concentration of wealth and income in Guatemala and El Salvador. Coffee did not develop as an export crop as in the other countries; the large land-owners did not consolidate their power as a ruling elite and did not appropriate as much land as their counterparts in El Salvador and Guatemala. Consequently land did not become a major issue until the 1950s, as a result of population growth and the expansion of other export crops. At the same time, land was more plentiful and, in 1962, 1972 and 1975, different governments responded to pressure from rural organisations by introducing modest agrarian reforms. They were also able to take advantage of large tracts of unused land still owned by the state to introduce colonisation schemes to ease land hunger among the peasants. Between 1962 and 1981 a total of 231,039 hectares was distributed to 53,806 peasant families.[11] These agrarian reforms, combined with the greater availability of land in Honduras, diluted social tensions in the rural areas which, in El Salvador and Guatemala, were the single most important contributing factor to the guerrilla wars of the 1980s.

Nicaraguan experience is not dissimilar. Growth, based on the diversification of agricultural exports, worked against the poor. Production of cotton expanded 120-fold between 1949 and 1955, and eventually cotton plantations came to occupy 40% of cultivated land. The accompanying expulsion of small farmers from their lands swelled the waged agricultural labour force by 180,000 seasonal cotton workers.[12] Some migrated to the towns and others were pushed to the agricultural frontier in the east where they hacked new smallholdings out of the forest. In 1973, of the 228,000 workers employed in the cotton harvest, only 26,000 had year-round employment. In 1972 1.4% of the total number of farms occupied 41.2% of the farmland. In that year, the average annual income of the poorest 50% of the rural population was $35.[13] Towards the end of the 1970s the UN Economic Commission for Latin America (ECLA) report classified 61.5% of the population as 'living in a state of poverty' and 80% of the rural population as 'living in a state of extreme poverty'.[14] In 1977 the wealthiest 5% of the population earned 28% of the total income while the poorest 50% received about 12%.[15] In the 1960s and 1970s, while national income nearly tripled, the rate of childhood malnutrition doubled.[16]

Costa Rica developed differently. There were no mineral resources and few native inhabitants to attract Spanish colonists. Land was relatively plentiful so that land ownership was less concentrated and rural workers surplus to the requirements of the coffee growers were able to open up new smallholdings beyond the central plateau, with the result that land was more evenly distributed in Costa Rica than in the neighbouring republics. Costa Rica, however, does not escape the general problems of poverty affecting Central America. In 1980 34.2% of the population were classified as living in a state of poverty, about half the average proportion in Central America as a whole.[17] By the 1960s the expansion of cattle-raising as part of government policies to reduce dependence on coffee as an export crop had used up all the unoccupied land, pushing peasants and their families back to the cities. These problems in the rural areas have not yet provoked political crisis. In 1971, however, one Costa Rican historian was already saying:

> The misery of the great majority of agricultural sharecroppers and tenants, small land-holders and labourers, is considerable. In recent years the demands of the peasants for land have been heard, and this struggle has, on several occasions, bordered on rebellion . . .

many have occupied latifundio land by force.[18]

The difficulties of Costa Rica, even before the economic crisis of 1979 to 1983, are reflected in the ECLA study which shows that between 1971 and 1977 the income of the poorest 20% of Costa Ricans declined at an annual rate of 1.4%.[19]

2. Political development

The violation of human rights is a consequence of the way in which this social and economic inequity has been defended by the economic elites, armies and security forces of Central America. They have been backed by successive US governments, whose concern with 'communism' has dominated all other considerations, leading to policies which have aggravated the injustices at the root of unrest in the region. The statistics of deaths, torture, disappearances and exile are staggering. 50,000 Nicaraguans were killed during the insurrection. Over 20,000 have been killed since 1979 in the contra war. Over 150,000 Guatemalans have been killed in the past 20 years, the vast majority of them peasants slaughtered by the armed forces. 60,000 Salvadoreans have been killed since 1979, most of them civilians killed by the security forces. In spite of their elections and civilian governments, the security forces of El Salvador and Guatemala continue to prey on their own people, enjoying an immunity from prosecution which has not been breached even in the most flagrant cases. The apparatus of state terror has been established in Honduras. Citizens have been tortured in clandestine prisons, killed and 'disappeared' by the security forces, though the cases are numbered in scores rather than the tens of thousands of El Salvador and Guatemala. In these countries killings continue, though in smaller numbers than at the beginning of the 1980s, and there is no prospect that the security forces who commit them can be brought under control or made accountable to civilian governments pledged to uphold human rights. Nor, at the same time, is there any prospect of radical reforms to correct the extreme social and economic inequity which has been described. The era of rapid economic growth has come to an end and the opportunities it might have provided for less painful change have been squandered by economic elites seemingly mesmerised by new possibilities of profit.

Guatemala was the first country to suffer from the combination of domestic reaction and US concern with communism in Central America. In 1954 a CIA coup overthrew the government of Jacobo Arbenz because it had included in its modest agrarian reform unused land belonging to the United Fruit Company. The legacy of violence left by the coup was recognised by the report of the Kissinger Commission on Central America, which acknowledged that '. . . politics became more divisive, violent and polarised than in neighbouring states.'[20] In the late 1960s a small guerrilla force led by disaffected army officers was countered by a massive military onslaught which killed an estimated 8,000 peasants. Throughout the 1970s, even as peasants were being encouraged by the government to join cooperatives, political leaders and community organisers were 'disappeared' from the streets of Guatemala City or gunned down by death squads.

Throughout the 1970s El Salvador was moving towards civil war. The military government, itself subservient to the country's economic elite, held elections but ensured through fraud that its candidate emerged victorious. Moderate reforming candidates for the presidency were kept out of power by rigged elections in 1972 and 1977. In 1976 the landowners, who constituted the majority in Congress, blocked a timid agrarian reform law proposed by their own military government, signalling that they would not willingly permit any reform that curtailed their own power and privilege. From 1976 onwards the government relied increasingly on terror and coercion.

In Nicaragua political and military power, as well as about a fifth of the wealth and productive assets of the country, were concentrated in the hands of the Somoza family. The increasing dissatisfaction of the business and agro-export sector with the dictatorship and Anastasio Somoza's stubborn attachment to power eventually led these groups to ally themselves with the revolutionaries. At the end of the 1970s Nicaragua was the only country in Central America where the Chambers of Commerce and business associations were not synonymous with the most recalcitrant right-wing parties. The result was a revolution, achieved at great human and material cost, which put in power a government pledged to correct the imbalance between the very rich and the poor, to making economic and social rights a reality.

As Nicaragua was beginning the task of post-revolutionary reconstruction in 1979 and 1980, El Salvador and Guatemala plunged into guerrilla war. There had been small guerrilla groups in both countries since the beginning of the 1970s but, apart from their ability to mount spectacular bank robberies and to kidnap for ransom prominent members of the oligarchy, they were largely ineffective as political movements. They had little support from peasants and urban workers. The energies of the union and peasant movements were put into peaceful protest, demonstrations and strikes. The peasant movements had grown out of community organisations started by priests and Catholic activists, and in the early 1970s the majority of trade unionists were linked to moderate reformist parties. The response of the authorities was extreme violence. In El Salvador demonstrators were fired on by the security forces. The intransigence and violence of the government brought the mass organisations — coalitions of unions, peasant federations, student organisations and other pressure groups — into contact with the guerrilla groups, which were competing for a base of support in the population.

In Guatemala towards the end of the 1970s a similar process took place. The guerrilla groups seemed to offer the only remaining alternative to activists in unions and political parties whose leaders had been murdered or forced into exile by a military government and a business elite determined to resist all pressure for change, which treated peaceful protest as if it were armed rebellion. On 21 June 1980 27 union leaders meeting at the headquarters of the CNT, a union grouping previously linked to the international Christian Democrat movement, were kidnapped by plain-clothes gunmen and never seen again. Sixteen priests and hundreds of catechists were killed.

3. Human rights

The guerrilla movements of El Salvador and Guatemala have not been extinguished, nor has there been any significant amelioration of the dire poverty and inequality out of which they were born. In El Salvador the FMLN guerrilla front has been driven back, but has countered the new firepower and technology of the armed forces by dividing into smaller units and reaching into new areas. The cost of the war since 1979 has been enormous. Over a million Salvadoreans have been forced to leave their homes: half of them live as refugees in neighbouring countries and the United States. The other half are displaced people, the more fortunate sheltered in church-run refuges or programmes, most simply eking out an existence in the slums of San Salvador. Since 1979 about 60,000 Salvadoreans have been killed as a result of political violence. Over 40,000 of the dead are non-combatant civilians killed by the security forces and the death squads, which are closely linked to them. These are minimum figures, including only known and documented cases. *Socorro Jurídico* and *Tutela Legal*, the two human rights groups which have worked with the Catholic archdiocese of San Salvador, had recorded over 37,086 killings by December 1984. The true figures, including deaths in the remote countryside, where verification is impossible, are higher. Some 4,500 people have 'disappeared' since 1979. The Catholic church too has been directly affected. Between 1977 and 1980 11 priests, including Archbishop Oscar Romero, were shot by gunmen, death squads or the security forces. Four US missionaries — two Maryknoll sisters, one

Ursuline nun and one lay missionary — were raped and shot by a National Guard platoon. The killing goes on. According to *Tutela Legal*, in 1985 there were 240 'targeted killings' by death squads, the army, security forces and civil defence militias. 371 civilians were killed in indiscriminate attacks by the army, and 1,045 people were killed in the course of military operations, the majority of whom are believed to have been civilians, but could not be definitely identified as such because *Tutela Legal* was unable to conduct on-site investigations. There were 81 cases of disappearance attributable to death squads or government forces. During the same period there were 128 deaths — targeted, indiscriminate and from land mines — attributed to the guerrilla forces.[21] As Americas Watch comments,

> There are few places elsewhere where some 1,900 political killings and disappearances a year — approximately 90 per cent of them at the hands of armed forces ostensibly controlled by a civilian democratic government — would be considered routine. In El Salvador, however, where the number of killings reached a high of some 13,000 in 1981, the comparison to what went before has blunted the impact of current figures.[22]

In 1986, *Tutela Legal* documented 18 cases of disappearance and 123 killings attributed to the army, security forces, civil defence forces and death squads. 39 murders are attributed to the guerrilla forces.[23]

In Guatemala it is estimated that since 1980 between 50,000 and 75,000 persons have been killed or 'disappeared' in response to an insurgency which at its peak involved 6,000 combatants and 260,000 civilian supporters. Another assessment of the scale of the killing is provided by a study commissioned by the Juvenile Division of the Supreme Court, which estimated that between 150,000 and 200,000 orphaned children had lost one or both parents.[24] Despite the election of a civilian president in December 1985, killing and disappearances continue. In June and July 1986, 31 kidnappings or disappearances were reported. Seven of the victims were subsequently released or found alive. 228 killings were reported by the Guatemalan press, of which 64 were attributed to common criminals.[25] By implication, the remainder had some political motivation. It is also reasonable to assume that other killings, especially those in the remote countryside, are not reported in the press. In a later report Americas Watch and the British Parliamentary Human Rights Group concluded: 'We are convinced . . . that a significant number of politically motivated killings and disappearances continue to take place in Guatemala, and little effort is made to punish those responsible.'[26]

In both El Salvador and Guatemala the effect of this violence has been to circumscribe the area of politics seen as legitimate and to intimidate dissent. Humanitarian organisations working in both countries are finding it increasingly difficult to work independently and are being forced by the authorities to assist government-run programmes in which control of the civilian population and counter-insurgency are the main objectives.

Honduras has largely escaped the excesses of its neighbours. Since 1980, however, the presence of thousands of Nicaraguan contras and a military obsession with subversion have introduced similar police and security practices. Up to 200 people may have been killed by the security forces in extra-judicial executions.[27] The Honduran Commission for Human Rights (CODEH) demanded an account of the fate of 147 people who were 'disappeared' by the security forces between 1979 and 1984. To date no satisfactory explanation has been provided by the authorities. In 1985 four Hondurans were 'disappeared' for political reasons and one Nicaraguan, in what may have been a case of forced recruitment by the contras.[28]

This account has concentrated on the most extreme forms of human rights violation, extra-judicial assassination and 'disappearance'. Torture has not been mentioned. It is still routine in Honduras, El Salvador and Guatemala. The effects on civil life of this period of prolonged bloodshed, which has not ended, are incalculable. Certainly political life is severely restricted. Public advocacy of the radical reforms that these countries need if they are to achieve equitable development is dangerous. Organisation to press for those reforms outside the established party system is almost suicidal. This is the background against which the Nicaraguan record must be set.

3. Nicaragua before 1979

1. US intervention

Nicaragua obtained its independence from Spain in 1821 after a short war of independence which liberated the whole of Central America, previously governed by Spain as one unit known as the Captaincy-General of Guatemala. Shortly afterwards, in 1823, President Monroe of the United States enunciated a set of principles, later known as the 'Monroe doctrine', a statement of intent on the part of the United States that no foreign intervention would be permitted in the Americas. This was directed at the European colonial powers. The two exceptions to the Monroe doctrine in Central America were the colony of British Honduras, now Belize, between the eastern frontier of Guatemala and the Caribbean, and the Atlantic coast area of Nicaragua, where British influence encouraged the emergence of an ill-defined territory maintaining commercial, political and cultural links with Britain but without any formal colonial status. British influence on the Atlantic Coast was formally brought to an end by the Treaty of Managua, signed in 1860 between the governments of the United Kingdom and Nicaragua, by which the Nicaraguan government agreed to the setting up of an autonomous Miskito territory on the coast in return for Britain's ceding of all rights over the area to Nicaragua. The terms of this treaty were never made effective but have been referred to by Miskito leaders in their discussions with the government of Nicaragua.

During the 19th century, politics in Nicaragua was dominated by the rivalry of the Conservative party, based in Granada, and the Liberal party in León. At the same time, US interest in the region was growing, together with the ability of the United States to impose its will on the region. The strategic importance of Nicaragua was demonstrated in 1849, when its connecting rivers and lakes made it the main route from the east to the west coast of the United States during the California gold rush, at a time when travel across the mainland of the United States was still hazardous and difficult. Then, in 1856, came the six-month presidency of the American soldier of fortune, William Walker, who, having made common cause with the Liberal government of the day against insurgent Conservatives, seized power for himself. This is an episode which understandably still rankles with Nicaraguan nationalists.

The building of the Panama Canal between 1904 and 1914 marks the beginning of real US intervention. It was the possibility of a second and rival canal being built in Nicaragua that focused US attention on Nicaragua. The US government was only too willing to aid Conservative rebels fighting against the Liberal president, José Santos Zelaya, and intervened directly in 1910 when two US citizens fighting with the Conservatives were captured and executed by the Zelaya government. After the US marines had installed Adolfo Díaz, the new government signed a treaty declaring that Nicaragua would never build an inter-oceanic canal. The US marines remained in Nicaragua as an occupying force until 1918 but returned two years later when the Liberals once again appeared to be gaining the upper hand in a war of rebellion waged on the Atlantic coast. In 1928 a second treaty transferred San Andrés island, off Nicaragua's Atlantic Coast, to Colombia as a sort of consolation prize from the United States, which had engineered the secession of the Republic of Panama from Colombia for the building of the canal.

2. Sandino

In 1926 Augusto César Sandino, returning to Nicaragua from Mexico, joined the Liberal forces fighting for Juan Bautista Sacasa. He had no previous military experience. For the previous five years he had worked for American companies in Honduras, Guatemala and Mexico. At that time Mexico was a ferment of revolutionary and radical ideas, and it seems likely that Sandino was influenced by what he learnt during his years abroad. Sandino adopted the red and black flag of the Spanish anarchists, saying that the colours were the symbols of liberty or death. Certainly he was a fierce nationalist. He had been with the Liberals for only six months when, in May 1927, they signed a truce with Henry Stimson, the personal envoy of President Coolidge. Because the truce allowed US troops to remain on Nicaraguan soil, Sandino angrily rejected offers of personal advantage which were made to persuade him to accept the armistice. In September Sandino formally announced the formation of the 'Army in Defence of National Sovereignty' (*Ejército Defensor de la Soberanía Nacional*). In spite of the participation of US troops and the use of planes to strafe and bomb rural areas — Ocotal, in northern Nicaragua, was the first town in the western hemisphere to suffer bombing from the air — Sandino waged a successful guerrilla campaign which continued until the US troops withdrew in February 1933. The removal of US troops from Nicaragua was Sandino's principal aim, and he duly laid down his weapons and disbanded his guerrilla force.

Sandino retired to the north of the country and founded an agricultural settlement at Wiwilí with a group of his most faithful soldiers. He remained an important national figure, however, and did not withdraw from politics. In the 12 months after the signing of the armistice he visited President Sacasa three times to express his growing concern about the behaviour of the US-trained National Guard under Colonel Anastasio Somoza, appointed commander-in-chief by the occupying forces before they left Nicaragua. On his third visit Sandino and his two principal lieutenants were murdered on the orders of Somoza.

3. The Somoza dynasty

As commander-in-chief of the National Guard, in 1934 Anastasio Somoza was already the most powerful man in Nicaragua. In 1936 he ousted President Sacasa in a bloodless coup and set up the family dictatorship which lasted until July 1979. At that time Somoza was simply another dictator in a region ruled by military dictators. In El Salvador, Honduras and Guatemala they had assumed power in the early 1930s to protect the interests of the local land-owning elites against the threat of political unrest after the collapse of coffee prices during the great depression.

Somoza took advantage of World War II to pass anti-Nazi legislation and confiscate the property of German settlers. After the attack on Pearl Harbor he declared war on Japan, Italy and Germany. He overcame without difficulty the wave of enthusiasm for democracy which swept through Central America at the end of the war. Ruling the country like a feudal baron, he used threats and bribes, imprisonment and exile to obtain the political cooperation of the Nicaraguan political elite. The family fortune grew because Somoza used his position to extort concessions, special payments and property from business rivals. The National Guard itself at all levels became a byword for corruption and extortion.

After the assassination of Anastasio Somoza in 1956, his elder son Luis took over with his younger brother, Anastasio (Tachito), retaining control of the National Guard. Luis, like his father, was politically astute, combining concern for the family fortune with the same mixture of repression, bribery and occasional leniency towards opposition activists in Nicaragua and consistent flattery of the US

government. Anastasio, who became president when Luis died of a
heart attack in April 1967, was more crude. He filled senior positions in
the National Guard and the administration with people whose only
qualification was their personal loyalty to him, stripping the last
vestiges of professionalism from government.

The political party of the Somoza family was the Liberal Nationalist
party. Under old Anastasio Somoza every public employee had to be a
member of the party. The traditional opposition party was the
Conservative party, joined in 1944 by the Independent Liberal Party
(*Partido Liberal Independiente* — PLI) and in 1957 by the Social Christian
Party (PSC). Throughout the Somoza era there were periodic
rebellions, none of which came near to success. Indeed, in a country
where politics was conducted in and between family clans, most of
these rebellions were detected in advance by the National Guard.
None of them aroused any popular enthusiasm even when their
success depended on such support, such as the 'Movimiento de Olama
y Mollejones', an expeditionary force launched from Costa Rica in June
1959 which was supposed to spark off a popular rebellion. One
hundred and twelve of the 114-strong force were captured by the
National Guard after only a few hours in Nicaragua. None of these
rebellions resulted in fierce repression. Most of the participants came
from well-connected families, and were punished by only brief spells
of imprisonment or exile.

Throughout this time the Somozas routinely rigged elections to
maintain themselves in power. The Conservative party protested by
boycotting the elections of 1957 and 1963, a traditional response to the
hopeless corruption of the democratic process. The response of the
Somozas was to tempt cooperative members of the opposition into
accepting those places in Congress, a third in all, which were reserved
for the opposition.

4. Opposition to Somoza

The FSLN was founded in 1961, one of several Latin American guerrilla
movements formed in the surge of enthusiasm which followed the
Cuban revolution. Its early history, like that of the others, is one
setback after another. In 1967 it was all but wiped out. In the 1970s,
however, the Sandinistas began to win over and organise the rural
population, the urban workers and the students.

These early setbacks forced the Sandinistas to change their tactics,
making them aware of the importance of mass organisation and its
techniques. This brought them into contact and, eventually,
cooperation with those sectors of the Catholic Church which also
stressed the importance of critical awareness and organisation among

the poor as essential steps in the building of a better society. The Sandinistas, however, did not reject violence, which they saw as necessary to hasten the decomposition of a regime completely bereft of moral authority.

After the earthquake of 23 December 1972, which devastated Managua and killed 20,000 people, Somoza, his friends and the National Guard treated emergency aid from abroad as one more opportunity for personal enrichment, definitively alienating the sectors of the ruling class that had grudgingly tolerated his father and elder brother. Two years later, on 27 December 1974, the FSLN raided a party being given by the Minister of Agriculture and took the guests hostage. These included several relatives of Somoza, who was eventually persuaded to negotiate the release of the hostages in return for the freeing of Sandinista prisoners, the publication of an FSLN manifesto and payment of a US$5m ransom. A state of siege was declared immediately afterwards and the National Guard mounted a campaign against the FSLN in the mountains of Matagalpa the brutality of which inflamed popular hatred of the regime. The Capuchin missionaries working in the area compiled a dossier of the National Guard's atrocities which was made public by the Catholic Bishops' Conference.

Opposition to Somoza gathered momentum throughout the 1970s. The brutality of the National Guard's counter-insurgency campaign in the north of the country polarised opinion against the regime. Both the traditional bourgeois opposition and the Catholic Church lost patience with Somoza and joined the growing opposition movement. At the same time the FSLN, though divided between three constituent 'tendencies', became more effective and succeeded in recruiting some of the most able and idealistic members of the student movement, many of them the sons and daughters of the traditional elite. Abroad the Carter administration in the United States, which assumed office in January 1977, made Nicaragua a proving ground for its human rights policies, removing a source of support that had been crucial to the Somoza family since the 1930s.

In 1977 Amnesty International published a report on Nicaragua which was a comprehensive indictment of human rights violations under the state of siege. The report repeated the accusations of church sources that many *campesinos* had been shot in cold blood by military forces and that torture was routine and widespread.[1]

In 1974 Pedro Joaquín Chamorro founded the Democratic Liberation Union (UDEL), bringing together Conservative and Liberal groups which rejected the political rules of the game set by the Somozas. In 1977 the 'Group of Twelve' (*Los Doce*), representing the most influential sectors of Nicaraguan society, formally endorsed the FSLN, saying that it should be included in any solution to the Nicaraguan crisis. The assassination of Pedro Joaquín Chamorro in January 1978, by killers who were linked immediately in the popular mind to Somoza, was another turning point, sparking off massive popular unrest and persuading yet more upper-class families that they should join the opposition. In 1978, the Broad Opposition Front (FAO) was founded, including both UDEL and the Twelve, but its insistence on negotiations with Somoza and willingness to make concessions destroyed its credibility and gave the political initiative to the FSLN and its allies.

These political manoeuvres took place against a background of increasing violence. The use of the state of siege regulations by the Somoza government to crush the opposition inflamed the population against the regime, confirming the argument long advanced by the FSLN that the dictatorship could only be dislodged by force. Although the FSLN continued to mount hit-and-run raids against police posts, the most significant bursts of insurrectionary violence were largely spontaneous outbreaks of popular hatred against the regime.

In February 1978 a ceremony naming a small square after Pedro Joaquín Chamorro in the *barrio* of Monimbó in Masaya became a riot against the National Guard and then an insurrection of the entire neighbourhood which was crushed two weeks later when the Guard attacked in force with heavy weapons. Later that month there were similar rebellions in Diriamba and León.

On 23 August 1978 the FSLN occupied the Congress building in downtown Managua, taking nearly 2,000 hostages. In the subsequent negotiations Somoza agreed to release 60 political prisoners, publish a FSLN manifesto calling for popular insurrection and provide a US$500,000 ransom. The occupation of the Congress building forestalled a National Guard coup against Somoza.[2] Its success and the popular reaction to it convinced the Sandinistas that the insurrectionary strategy could work. The business strike organised by COSEP (Superior Council of Private Enterprise) flared into insurrections in several major cities in September and October. This time there was decisive Sandinista participation complementing spontaneous rejection of the regime.

The horrifying response of the Somoza government was documented in a report published by the Inter-American Commission on Human Rights in November 1978. National Guard detachments, helicopters and planes shelled and bombed the cities into submission, attacking the general population rather than the guerrilla fighters who were besieging the National Guard garrisons. The conclusions of the report are a catalogue of gross human rights violations.[3]

Somoza held on for a further nine months. His stubborn attachment to power and the Carter administration's insistence that a new transitional government should include National Guard and Nationalist Liberal party representatives while excluding the FSLN served only to discredit the FAO negotiators and those who were hoping that a reformist, rather than a revolutionary, government could be salvaged from the ruins of 'somocismo'. The result was unconditional victory for the FSLN and its allies on 19 July 1979.

The insurrection in Nicaragua, though comparatively brief and conducted in spasms from August 1978 to July 1979, was costly in human and material terms. 50,000 people were killed. These figures, however, do not tell the whole story. The savagery of the National Guard was such that its members will be remembered with loathing for many years to come. Torture, mutilation and summary execution, especially of young men taken from the streets of the popular *barrios*, were commonplace.

National income fell by one-third in 1978 and 1979. Even the most optimistic forecasts predicted that it would take Nicaragua ten years to recover the level of economic activity achieved in 1977. Even if Nicaragua had enjoyed peace and the goodwill of its neighbours and the United States, reconstruction would have been difficult enough.

4. A Country at War

1. Introduction

Nicaragua has been at war almost since the insurrection of July 1979. At first it was a war of skirmishes and raids carried out by former members of the National Guard who had fled to Honduras. It is estimated that 3,000 former members of the National Guard reached Honduras, establishing camps and maintaining themselves as a structured military force. Nevertheless they were demoralised, the general attitude towards the new government in Nicaragua was euphoric and the Carter administration in the United States, as distinct from the CIA, gave them no encouragement. The new government treated the attacks as the dying echoes of Somocista resistance rather than as the first manifestation of an organised counter-revolutionary movement. The highest priority of the new government was reconstruction and bringing the revolution home to the ordinary people of Nicaragua as real and palpable improvements in their lives.

Of the 59 literacy volunteers who died during the National Literacy Crusade between March and July 1980, only nine were killed by anti-government elements in what the Nicaraguans at that time described as political assassinations. This figure, low by subsequent standards, gives an indication of the relative security of the Nicaraguan rural areas one year after the revolution. The volunteers were unarmed and were posted to the some of the most remote communities in Nicaragua. More volunteers were killed by drowning (19), illness (10) and road accidents (10).[1]

The election of Ronald Reagan as President of the United States in November 1980 signalled that the new government of Nicaragua would not be able to count on the neutrality of the United States. The Republican National Convention Platform of July 1980 deplored the '. . . Marxist Sandinista takeover of Nicaragua and the Marxist attempts to destabilise El Salvador, Guatemala and Honduras . . .', promising to '. . . support the efforts of the Nicaraguan people to establish a free and independent government' and to return to '. . . the fundamental principle of treating a friend as a friend and self-proclaimed enemies as enemies, without apology.'

In January 1981 the FMLN guerrilla movement in El Salvador launched a large-scale offensive in an attempt to spark off a national insurrection before the new US administration was able to develop a coherent policy. To many Central Americans, including the Sandinistas, this armed rebellion was a justified response to the gross and systematic human rights abuses of a government which had lost all claim to legitimacy. The US government, however, seized on the evident Nicaraguan sympathy for the FMLN in El Salvador, and on some material help from Nicaragua, to accuse the Nicaraguans of 'exporting their revolution'. In March 1981 the Reagan administration suspended credit for Nicaraguan purchases of wheat from the United States and authorised the CIA to undertake covert actions against Nicaragua. In September a loan of US$7mn from the US Agency for International Development was suspended. In October the Senate approved an amendment stipulating that all US aid to Nicaragua should go to the private sector. In November President Reagan personally approved a plan calling for a CIA-administered US$19mn programme of military aid, to be administered by the CIA, to build a 500-strong paramilitary force for attacks on targets in Nicaragua.

Between 1981 and 1986, the contras received approximately US$100mn in officially recognised US economic and military aid. The real figure is thought to be much higher. Congressional investigations into the secret sale of US weapons to Iran in 1985 have revealed that the proceeds from the transactions, estimated at US$12mn, were used illegally to channel support to the contras. Saudi Arabia has contributed over US$30mn to the contras, possibly at the personal request of President Reagan. In addition, the Sultan of Brunei was prevailed upon by Assistant Secretary of State Elliott Abrams to contribute US$10mn, which, as it turns out, never reached the contras, having been deposited in the wrong Swiss bank account.[2] Israel is also reported to have shipped smaller quantities of weapons to them. All these transactions took place at a time when the US Congress maintained a ban on official US aid to the contras. In July 1986, however, Congress approved a further US$70mn in military aid and $30mn in 'humanitarian' aid. Estimates of the funds available to the CIA for administering this aid, directing the contra war effort and training are as high as $300mn.

2. The contras

The contras are Nicaraguan insurgents, with bases in Honduras and some presence in Costa Rica, who are fighting to overthrow the Sandinista government. Initially they were composed almost entirely of former officers and soldiers in Somoza's National Guard, who formed an organisation based in Honduras called the 15 September Legion. Since 1981 they have managed to recruit other Nicaraguans, but their military structure is still based on a nucleus of former National Guard personnel. The FDN (*Fuerzas Democráticas Nicaragüenses*), which was formed as an alliance between the 15 September Legion and the Nicaraguan Democratic Union (UDN), is the major contra military force. With the help and encouragement of the Reagan administration, it has absorbed lesser, rival organisations. Those that have refused to cooperate with the FDN, such as Edén Pastora's *Frente Revolucionario Sandinista* (FRS), have been starved of funds and forced to disband.

The commander-in-chief of the FDN is Enrique Bermúdez, a former colonel in the National Guard. The officer corps of the FDN is staffed almost entirely by former members of the Guard. A report produced by the Arms Control and Foreign Policy Caucus — a bipartisan group consisting of liberal members of the House and the Senate — which was released in April 1985 with the title *Who are the contras?* concluded that 46 of the 48 positions in the FDN military leadership were held by former National Guardsmen. This is strenuously denied by the US State Department, but even its documents acknowledge that former National Guard officers occupy five out of the seven posts in the FDN 'strategic command'.[3] Other former Guardsmen with positions of conspicuous responsibility in the FDN include Armando López, a former captain in the National Guard who now has responsibility for FDN logistics, and Ricardo Lau, who is both bodyguard and adviser to Bermúdez and is known to have participated in assassinations and torture sessions. Lau was accused by Col. Roberto Santibáñez, a former chief of military intelligence in El Salvador, of recruiting former National Guardsmen to assassinate Archbishop Romero.[4]

Formally, the FDN is under the political direction of the *Unión Nacional Opositora* (UNO), a political front cobbled together by the Reagan administration and headed until early 1987 by Arturo Cruz, Alfonso Robelo and Adolfo Calero, the political head of the FDN. Calero resigned from UNO on 20 February 1987 in response to Cruz's almost continual threats to resign in protest against the ineffectiveness of UNO as the policy-making body of the contras. Calero, however, did not relinquish control of the FDN, further undermining UNO's ability to control the contras. Cruz himself finally resigned on 9 March 1987.

The record of the contras in the field, as opposed to their official professions of democratic faith, is one of consistent and bloody abuse of human rights, of murder, torture, mutilation, rape, arson, destruction and kidnapping. Despite repeated denials that such tactics are official policy, the contras have not modified their behaviour nor disciplined any units for committing atrocities. According to Edgar Chamorro, a disillusioned former contra who gave evidence to the International Court of Justice during 1985 in the course of Nicaragua's suit against the government of the United States,

> FDN units would arrive at an undefended village, assemble all the residents in the town square and then proceed to kill — in full view of the others — all persons suspected of working for the Nicaraguan government or the FSLN, including the police, local militia members, party members, health workers, teachers, and farmers from government-sponsored cooperatives. In this atmosphere, it was not difficult to persuade those able-bodied men left alive to return with the FDN units to their base camps in Honduras and enlist in the force.[5]

Contra atrocities have been investigated and documented by Americas Watch, Amnesty International, the Washington Office on Latin America and independent US lawyers who have gathered testimony from witnesses and survivors of contra raids. Attacks on civilians have continued in 1986:

> On 16 February near Somotillo, Chinandega, a pickup truck carrying 14 unarmed women and children was ambushed by contra troops, who first manually detonated a Claymore mine and then opened fire. The driver of the truck, Maurice Demierre, a 29-year-old Swiss agronomist just completing a three-year term with the organisation 'Brothers without Frontiers', was killed, as were four of the women — Rosa Castellón, 66, Etelvina Lagos, 25, Valentina Mairena, 70, and Adilia Guillén, 28. Another passenger, 25-year old Pilar Betancourt Castellón, who had been paralysed from the neck down in the ambush, died on 26 March. Thirteen-year old Xochitl del Socorro Moncada, who was hurt in the ambush, stated that she heard an attacker say, 'It's too bad they're only women.'[6]

On the evening of 23 April 1986 four contras in uniform came to a general store in Agua Amarilla, Department of Zelaya. They burned down the store and abducted the owner of the store, José Rodríguez, aged 73, his 15-year old daughter and a woman teacher, aged 20, who had been living with the family. Mr Rodríguez's body was found the following morning about 500 yards from the house. His throat had been cut. At the end of June there had been no news of the kidnapped women. The reporters, who took a sworn statement from José Rodríguez's widow, conclude:

> This case illustrates the . . . strategy of the contras of targetting civilians who cooperate with the government. Mr. Rodríguez was vulnerable to contra vengeance in this regard both because he allowed a teacher to stay in his house and because, even though his store was privately owned, he helped distribute government-regulated provisions. The day before the contras came, he had received a large shipment of goods which had not yet been sold.[7]

On 24 May, near San José de Bocay, Jinotega, a Toyota pickup truck carrying teachers and health workers returning from a vaccination campaign against polio and measles struck an anti-tank mine, killing nine of the 13 passengers. Ambrosio Mogorrón, a Spanish nurse, was among the victims. The occupants of the truck were armed and in uniform because, as a survivor stated, 'We were carrying arms because we have to. If the contra find an unarmed government worker, they kill him.' On 3 July 32 people, including 12 women and 12 children, were killed when the lorry in which they were travelling was blown up by an anti-tank mine planted in the road between San José de Bocay and Jinotega.[8] Since the mine was placed in the only access road to San José de Bocay, it was almost inevitable that its victims would be civilian rather than military. On 20 October 1986 a mine planted in the road destroyed a second, privately-owned passenger lorry one kilometre south of Pantasma, killing six and wounding 43. Those killed were the driver, four women, one child and Santos Alvarez, a deacon in the Pantasma Nazarene Church. Two other evangelical pastors were injured.

The use of mines by the contras, a relatively recent feature of the war, is a clear contravention of the laws of war. Unless detonated manually they are 'blind' weapons which explode under the first vehicle to detonate them. The contras have mined roads in the north of the country, making travel dangerous. Americas Watch documented seven incidents between May and October 1986 in which 42 civilians were killed and 45 injured, some being maimed for life. A government official estimated that between January and September 1986 12 anti-tank mines had exploded in Region 6 (Jinotega and Matagalpa) and a further 18 had been deactivated.[9] Soldiers have also been killed by mines but precise figures are not available.

On 19 July 1986 President Daniel Ortega said that in seven years the contra war had claimed 31,290 victims, 16,925 contras and 14,260 Nicaraguans who had been killed, wounded or kidnapped 'defending national sovereignty'. It is almost routine for contras to rape the women they encounter and abduct. As mentioned above, foreign aid workers have been among the victims of contra attacks. In May 1986 eight German volunteers were kidnapped by contras and held for 25 days after an attack on Jacinto Baca in which, according to the released volunteers, the contras killed men and women indiscriminately. The contras claimed that their release, arranged after negotiations with the West German government, was evidence of their respect for human rights.[10] After the kidnapping, however, Frank Arana, a spokesman for the FDN, announced that 'Any foreigner who voluntarily aids in development and reconstruction projects is considered the enemy'.[11] On 28 July three European aid workers and two Nicaraguans, both civilians, were killed when their jeep was ambushed by contras in Sompopera near Jinotega.[12]

Abuses by the contras have spread into Honduras where, near the border with Nicaragua, they control a 200-square mile area which they call 'New Nicaragua'. The Commission for Human Rights in Honduras (CODEH) has taken testimony from Honduran peasants living near the contra camps who say that the contras have kidnapped and murdered local people.[13] It is estimated that 3,000 Honduran peasant families (16,000 people) have had to leave the area, becoming refugees in their own country.[14] The Honduran Association of Coffee Growers (AHPROCAFE) has asked the government in vain to clear the area of contras and has threatened to sue the US government.[15]

One incident stands out because it demonstrates the deliberate use of atrocity by a large and organised contra unit under the command of a senior officer, known as Dimas or Dumas. Having captured ten Sandinista soldiers who had been defending the town and a school watchman who was armed, they assembled the townspeople in the square, threatening to burn down their houses if they did not attend. After a speech by Dumas the 11 were led away and shot. Subsequently, when their bodies were found, it was discovered that several of them had been mutilated. Olman Martínez, the town coordinator, was spared because several townspeople spoke up for him at the meeting in the square.[16]

The significance of this incident lies in the fact that the contra unit followed to the letter the advice of a CIA manual, specially written for them, which, among other things, gives precise instructions regarding the use of terror. The manual states:

> It is possible to neutralise carefully selected and planned targets, such as court judges, *mesta* judges, police and State Security officials, CDS chiefs etc. For psychological purposes it is absolutely necessary to take extreme precautions, and it is absolutely necessary to gather together the population affected, so that they will be

present, take part in the act, and formulate accusations against the oppressor.[17]

The International Court of Justice examined the manual and concluded in its judgment that:

. . . the United States of America, by producing in 1983 a manual entitled *'Operaciones sicológicas en guerra de guerrillas'*, and disseminating it to contra forces, has encouraged the commission by them of acts contrary to general principles of humanitarian law . . .[18]

This account has concentrated on gross abuses with multiple victims which are clearly related to contra military strategy. Most of those killed by the contras, however, fall victim to them in ones and twos. The strategy of terror implicit in the use of mines and public executions is faithfully implemented against them. In February 1987 a British priest working in Muelle de los Bueyes in Central Zelaya reported: 'Yesterday, [11 February], I learned that near Presilla village, the contras compelled a youth to sustain his older brother's head while that head was hacked off with a machete. The younger brother was freed to tell the tale.'[19]

A Commission for Human Rights (UNO-CDH) was set up by UNO in August 1985 in order to investigate human rights abuses allegedly committed by contra forces. According to Amnesty International, a representative of this commission claimed in May 1986 that it had investigated 36 cases of complaints and had applied sanctions in 33 of them. Of the 14 cases of which details are available, only one, a case of multiple rape, involves physical abuse against Nicaraguans during military operations. Eight cases relate to abuses against other contras and four to theft or pillage.[20] The report of the commission's investigation into the Cuapa incident contradicts the reports of journalists and Americas Watch in almost every respect and appears to be a deliberate attempt to falsify the events which took place. UNO-CDH published its report without having interviewed the contra commander responsible for the Cuapa operation. No human rights organisation has been able to detect any reduction in abuses by the contras since the UNO Commission for Human Rights was set up.

UNO-CDH was closed down in August 1986. In October and November a new group, ANPDH (*Asociación Nicaragüense Pro Derechos Humanos*) opened offices in Costa Rica and Honduras. The ANPDH claims that it is independent of any political group but was described by a US State Department official as the successor of UNO-CDH, and has an office in a contra base camp at Yamale in Honduras. Its first report was about an incident at El Níspero on 9 November 1986 in which a contra force attacked a cooperative settlement and, after overwhelming the three soldiers and one militia man defending the village, killed a one year old baby by slitting its throat and abducted two women and a baby in arms. Two other women and another one year old child were killed as was a third woman who had been in the guard post at the time of the attack. The ANPDH report exonerates the contra forces from any blame, claiming against all the evidence that special Sandinista troops sealed off the area after the attack and mutilated the victims.[21]

Human rights organisations which have monitored abuses committed by the contras have concentrated on abuses against civilians because they constitute violations against the rules of war. This may be necessary because the abuses, if proven, then constitute violations of accepted international standards. One consequence of this approach, however, is to admit the possibility of a 'clean' contra war, in which no abuses are committed and only legitimate military targets are attacked. The Nicaraguan government maintains that the war itself is illegitimate, not only or even principally because the contras commit human rights violations, but because the contras are surrogates for the present US administration, which has declared war on Nicaragua in all but name. The government sees its defence effort as the defence of national sovereignty against a foreign invader.

The gross abuses committed by the contra are clearly counter-productive as far as their international image is concerned. Nevertheless, the torture and killing of civilians and the disgusting mutilations of the bodies of victims have had the effect of terrorising the civilian population in those areas of the country where they operate. The consequences have been the disruption of government services and supplies, the displacement of large numbers of peasant farmers and their families, the creation of shortages and the undermining of production.

3. The consequences of war

The effect of the war on ordinary people has been disastrous. First are the casualties. The majority of the deaths reported are of members of the militia or regular armed forces. The contras, however, deliberately kill civilians in order to sow terror among the population and to disable government services in the rural areas where they have attempted to create a base of support. For the period 1 January to 11 July 1986, the government reported 123 civilian deaths, 116 Sandinista army deaths and 2,745 contra deaths.[22] For 1986 as a whole, the government has reported 1,100 civilians and foreign workers killed, wounded or kidnapped.[23]

International attention has focused on the atrocities committed by the contras. Supporters of the Sandinistas can point out that insurgents who commit such atrocities — and the contras have been behaving in this way for over five years — are improbable standard-bearers of a new age of tolerance, democracy and pluralism. The most important effect of the contra war on the nation as a whole, however, is the direct economic damage caused by the contras and the indirect effects on the economy. This touches all Nicaraguans and all regions of the country and its effects will continue to be felt for many years after the fighting has come to an end.

Shortages are felt at all levels. The armed forces absorb 45% of the production of boots and shoes and 24% of textile production, which together account for 10% of industrial production. 10% of the production of basic foods also goes to the armed forces. The effects of this diversion of resources to defence have been felt most keenly in the cities. Between 1983 and 1984 the volume of powdered milk — the form in which milk is generally distributed in Nicaragua — assigned to Managua fell by one third. Such difficulties are reflected in a very high rate of inflation, over 1,000% in 1986, a flourishing black market and a steep decline in the real value of earnings of the great majority of the population. The UN Economic Commission for Latin America has calculated that, in normal circumstances, without a war, the Nicaraguan economy would recover its 1977 level of activity by 1989. Instead, the Nicaraguans have seen their GDP barely maintain the level to which it sank in 1979 as the result of the damage caused by the war of insurrection.[24]

The city of Managua itself is a vivid demonstration of the consequences of the war. Between 1979 and 1985 the population doubled from under 600,000 to over 1,000,000. Migrants from other parts of the country have crowded into Managua as refugees from the war or drawn by the possibility of work in the flourishing and uncontrollable informal sector, where a market seller may earn many times the salary of skilled workers or professionals working in industry or government.

The number of Nicaraguans directly affected by the war includes the 100,000 people under arms, either serving in the regular armed forces (65,000 to 75,000) or in the militia (25,000 to 35,000), the 250,000 displaced from the war zones, and possibly 500,000 people who live in areas where the contras are active. The most direct contact for people living outside the war zones is conscription (*Servicio Militar Patriótico*), which affects young men between the ages of 17 and 25, who have to serve for two years in the armed forces. Thus it is through conscription and the difficulties in everyday life that the majority of Nicaraguan families experience the war.

In the war zones the situation is more dramatic. In 1985 in Region VI (Matagalpa-Jinotega), the contras burnt down or blew up 151 buildings of various sorts, 21 vehicles (5 jeeps, 6 lorries, 9 pick-up trucks and a motorbike), killed or stole 131 head of cattle and destroyed farm equipment and road-making machinery. 57 people were killed, 14 wounded and 21 people kidnapped in these attacks.[25]

According to a survey conducted by Instituto Juan XXIII, in Region VI there are 6,000 families (over 30,000 people) living in *asentamientos*, resettlement areas or communities, after fleeing or being moved from the war zones. The government or voluntary agencies have to provide all the basic infrastructure and services. And even here the people are not safe: contras attacked two communities in the last week of April 1986, wounding three people and causing thousands of dollars' worth of damage.

As intended, the contra war has particularly affected the government's ability to extend its social welfare programmes to peasant families in remote rural areas, many of whom, because of the isolation in which they have lived, were initially suspicious of the Sandinistas and their new-fangled ideas. In March 1986 Sister Hilaria Micheluzzi, the coordinator of the pharmacy of the parish of Waslala, covering 64 communities, reported:

Recently there was an epidemic of measles in the zone. The first cases appeared in Yaro at the end of 1985. The doctors tried to get there with the vaccinations. It is one day away by horse. During that time there was a small period of calm, and they were able to get there and vaccinate. However, the epidemic spread to other sectors that were of more difficult access, controlled by the contras. The situation became critical, and in March there were many deaths. In Cano Sucio there were 46 deaths in less than 20 days. The neighbouring communities suffered a lot, and the epidemic continues. In Yakumali, six children in one family died.

One cannot get there because of the aggression. The contras do not allow health personnel to enter. They accuse them of collaborating with the government. Not long ago there was a vaccination campaign but only the closest were reached. The community of La Posolera held vaccinations, and fifteen minutes afterwards, more or less, the attack from the contras occurred.

The people in the countryside live in very difficult conditions. They are controlled by the contras, who do not allow them to sell their harvest or go to the towns to buy sugar, salt, everything they do not have. So they eat beans, corn and yuca. This created a serious malnutrition problem that decreases the [human] organism's defences and worsens the crisis. Now, with the measles, with this malnutrition, and without vaccinations, we have an uncontrollable health problem that is causing deaths, including in the town where refugees from the war are constantly arriving. This is the first time that we have seen a measles epidemic in my five years here.[26]

Large numbers of people have fled to safer areas, abandoning their crops and livestock, and the government has forced people to move, both to protect lives, and to clear certain zones of civilian population so as to deny the contras the possibility of using the local farmers as a source of supply, and eventually, of forming ties with the civilian population. The contra campaign of harassment and terror thus forms part of a wider strategy, the main purpose of which is to weaken the economy, provoking crippling shortages and such discontent that it is impossible for the Nicaraguan government effectively to mobilise the country for defence.

5. States of Emergency

1. Introduction

Nicaragua has been governed under states of emergency of varying degrees of severity for all but 16 months of the period since the revolution. Immediately after the insurrection the government declared a state of emergency which remained in force until 29 April 1980. On 9 September 1981 a 'state of social and economic emergency' was declared. In December 1981 a state of emergency was imposed in northern Zelaya, the northern Atlantic Coast region. In March 1982 the state of emergency was extended to the whole country, suspending all the civil rights which may be suspended according to the Statute of Rights and Guarantees of Nicaraguans. The rights suspended included the rights of *habeas corpus* and not to be arbitrarily detained in cases involving national security, and the rights to the freedoms of expression, assembly and movement, and to strike. The rights guaranteed unconditionally by Article 49 of the Statute include the rights to life and to physical, psychological and moral integrity, the right not to be subjected to cruel, inhuman or degrading punishment and not to be punished by retrospective laws, and the right to freedom of thought, conscience and religion. These guarantees are repeated in the new constitution. In making such guarantees the Nicaraguan statute follows exactly the wording of the International Convention on Civil and Political Rights.

Although the state of emergency regulations give the government sweeping powers, they have been used with discretion and the severity of their application has varied in response to the perceived contra threat and the political moment. During the pre-election period, from August to November 1984, there was a gradual relaxation of the state of emergency, enabling opposition parties to function normally. Prior censorship was not removed altogether, but the amount of censored material in *La Prensa* was significantly reduced. This milder application of the state of emergency was maintained until 15 October 1985, when a new state of emergency was declared, giving the security services wider powers of investigation and detention and further curbing strikes and the freedoms of speech and association. In November, however, the National Assembly amended the terms of the emergency decree, limiting the restriction on freedom of movement to war zones, and the restriction of freedom of expression to matters concerning military and economic affairs considered prejudicial to national security. Public meetings, demonstrations and strike actions were permitted with prior authorisation. *Habeas corpus* was restored in non-political cases. As a result of these amendments the scope of the new state of emergency is not significantly different from the one already in force.

The states of emergency, with their varying degrees of severity, reflect the Nicaraguan government's perception of the threat posed by the contra war. The purpose of the first state of emergency was to give the government the necessary powers to maintain order during the initial post-revolutionary period. The state of emergency imposed in northern Zelaya in December 1981 was a response to a series of raids from Honduras by Miskito anti-government guerrilla forces allied with the FDN, the most important contra force, which was at that time beginning to operate as a structured counter-revolutionary group with support from the United States.

Many states have responded to external threats or domestic terrorism with legislation which abridges the rights of people suspected of political offences and amends trial procedures. Moreover, countries with a recent history of dictatorship, such as the Federal Republic of Germany and Italy, have laws limiting the rights of those who profess certain ideologies. Emergency laws raise three major issues:

1. Are the powers which they give to the security forces and the curtailment of civil liberties proportional to the threat posed from abroad or by domestic terrorism? The question that this raises in Nicaragua is: how serious is the threat posed by the contra war?

2. Are the powers granted to the police, the security forces and the courts by the emergency laws directed towards the ends for which they are intended? Are these powers directed only against the contras and their supporters? Are other forms of opposition considered illegitimate?

3. Do the security services and other departments of state themselves observe the limitations on their activities imposed by the emergency laws? Do they respect the fundamental rights guaranteed unconditionally by the Statute of Rights and Guarantees?

Given the nature of the conflict in Nicaragua, there are not necessarily cut and dried answers to these questions, especially 1 and 2. Government and opposition give directly opposed answers.

2. Treatment of Somocista prisoners

The final collapse of the Somoza regime on 19 July 1979 left the country in chaos. Leaders of guerrilla units became *de facto* civil and military authorities overnight. Nicaragua's first state of emergency was a natural measure in a country where elements of the National Guard remained at large and where groups of revolutionary fighters linked only tenuously with the FSLN retained their weapons.

In spite of the bitter fighting and atrocities committed by Somoza's forces during the final weeks of the insurrection, there was relatively little revenge killing. One of the first acts of the new government was to abolish the death penalty. Grave abuses, however, did occur, but were numbered in tens rather than hundreds. The murder and clandestine burial of at least 18 detainees held in La Pólvora prison in Granada in July 1979 was proved beyond all doubt. The commander of the prison was dismissed and himself detained in August.[1] In March 1983, however, the Granada District judge found that it was not possible 'to determine, based on the evidence, that Marvin González Ruiz, 'Wilmer' [the gaol commander], was legally responsible for the events under investigation.'[2] The Permanent Commission for Human Rights, which is hostile to the government, published a list of 419 people who had been reported as having disappeared following detention between July and December 1979. 301 of these alleged disappearances occurred in July 1979,[3] when order had not been fully restored and the new government had not been able to disarm the less disciplined units which had participated in the insurrection.

The new government acted swiftly and decisively to prevent and punish violent abuses against alleged former government collaborators. Amnesty International concluded '. . . The evidence indicates that deaths of those detained by revolutionary forces, and unconfirmed detentions, virtually ceased after September 1979.'[4] Certainly the government's claim that it was necessary to set up an expeditious judicial procedure to try the alleged perpetrators of crimes committed by the former regime has a basis in fact. There was enormous popular ill-feeling against the National Guard and 'somocistas' in general. It is also true that the task of trying the *reos somocistas* was quite beyond the normal judicial system, as it then was, using existing legislation. This has been acknowledged by the Supreme Court which nevertheless argued at the time against the setting up of a system of special courts, urging that the number of ordinary judges should be increased to deal with the extra work load created by the large number of defendants.[5]

In the event, the government opted to set up a system of special courts (*Tribunales Especiales de Justicia*). These were created by Decree 185 on 5 December 1979 and functioned until 19 February 1981, when they were dissolved. They consisted of nine special courts and three appeal courts. A special prosecutor was appointed with a staff of nine.

At the time of the insurrection and during the following weeks between 7,000 and 8,000 former members of the National Guard and civilian supporters of the previous regime were taken into custody. 6,310 were tried by the Special Courts. 1,760 were pardoned or had their cases dismissed, 229 were acquitted and 4,331 received prison sentences.[6] At the end of World War II the French government charged 4,598 people with espionage and treason, of whom 756 were condemned to death.[7]

The procedure of the special courts has been criticised on the grounds that the normal standards of evidence were relaxed, that there was not time to prepare an effective defence and that the sentencing policy varied wildly between the different courts. The courts treated the National Guard itself as a criminal organisation, membership of which was accepted as proof of crimes committed without specific evidence being produced in court. The National Guard was described as a 'criminal organisation which showed supreme indifference to human dignity, especially with regard to prisoners of war, who were degraded and humiliated by virtue of their condition as prisoners'. The prosecutor affirmed in one case that 'The prisoner, by his conscious and voluntary membership in the ranks of the National Guard, endorsed, consented to and participated in the commission of crimes committed by the organisation referred to.'[8]

The special courts, however, faced great difficulties. One court president complained that it was impossible to prove the guilt of someone who tortured then killed a hooded victim and then disposed of all the witnesses. Defendant after defendant claimed that they had had only innocuous responsibilities within the National Guard. If he believed them all, the court president said, the National Guard was a body composed exclusively of cooks, gardeners and bricklayers. All the accused claimed that they had deserted during the last two months of the previous regime, when some of the worst atrocities took place. One driver, a member of the National Guard since 1978, claimed that he had no idea of what was going on because he was illiterate and did not read the papers, was too tired to listen to the radio when he got home and could not hear what the occupants of his bus were talking about because he could not hear them above the noise of the engine. A sergeant-major with ten years' service said that he was in the band and never left the barracks.[9]

One of the first tasks of the government-funded National Commission for the Protection and Promotion of Human Rights (*Comisión Nacional de Protección y Promoción de los Derechos Humanos* — CNPPDH), set up in June 1980, was to make recommendations under the Clemency Law (*Ley de Gracia*), passed in November 1981, which allowed for the review of sentences pronounced by the special courts. The recommendations were sent to the Council of State for endorsement which passed them to the Junta for implementation. This itself depended on the political moment. The CNPPDH has stated that some pardons were delayed after a major contra attack. It is known that some of those released under the Clemency Law have joined the contra forces. The Clemency Law did not provide for a review of the evidence or the conduct of the cases which led to conviction but allowed for a recommendation of pardon to be made on the basis of the behaviour of the prisoner. The CNPPDH, however, has stated that it did recommend some pardons as a result of what it considered glaring miscarriages of justice.

In July 1986 Tomás Borge, the Minister of the Interior, said that of the 4,331 *reos somocistas* who received prison sentences, some 2,157 remained in prison, the remainder having been pardoned or released on the completion of their sentences.[10] Since 56% of the prisoners received sentences of over ten years, this demonstrates that at least some 260 of those prisoners serving longer sentences have been released. At the end of January 1987 the government announced pardons for 300 prisoners, some of whom were former members of the National Guard, tried and imprisoned after the insurrection.

3. Human rights under the state of emergency

The right to life
Despite allegations to the contrary, there is no policy of killing or 'disappearing' political opponents or contras. In the seven years since the revolution there have been incidents in which people have been killed by the army or security forces. Many of these crimes have been investigated and those responsible have been punished. Cases in which those who were responsible received exemplary punishment include the sentencing of an army commander to 44 years' imprisonment — in spite of the fact that the maximum prison sentence in Nicaragua is 30 years — and 12 subordinates to terms of imprisonment of up to 14 years in 1984 for what the military prosecutor described as a 'reign of terror' in Pantasma, in the Jinotega region near the Honduran border. Their catalogue of crimes included at least six extra-judicial executions and possibly four disappearances.[11]

The two most important cases of extra-judicial executions by the Nicaraguan army or the security forces were on the Atlantic Coast. In December 1981 a group of 17 Miskito civilians were shot at Leimus in northern Zelaya, apparently in reprisal for an attack on an army unit in which several Sandinista soldiers were killed. Reports of these killings were first published by Americas Watch in May 1982.[12] The response of the government was to commission an investigation. The findings of the investigation, however, have never officially been made public. According to the Lawyers Committee for International Human Rights, those responsible for the Leimus massacre were included in the amnesty granted to all Miskito prisoners.[13] A brief report by a government official is included in the Ministry of the Interior documents published by the US State Department (see below p.51). This account, by Sub-Lieutenant Raúl Castro González of the Ministry of the Interior, indicates that those who participated in the shootings were gaoled but released six months later on the orders of Comandante Joaquín Cuadra, the commander-in-chief of the armed forces. The second case is that of 69 Miskito civilians who were detained by the Nicaraguan army or security forces in the Puerto Cabezas area between July and September 1982 and were allegedly executed by their captors. The government has not identified or punished those responsible but has implicitly acknowledged responsibility by paying a small pension to the families of some of the victims.[14] More detailed accounts of these incidents and the subsequent investigations appear in Chapter 9.

The fact that there have not been any further atrocities on the Atlantic Coast, such as the Río Leimus and Puerto Cabezas killings, is to be welcomed. This, however, does not excuse the Nicaraguan government from providing a full and public account of these incidents, as they have been asked to do by several human rights organisations.

Three other cases are particularly controversial because they formed part of the background to the congressional vote on contra aid in 1986. In March Bishop Vega of Juigalpa denounced three cases of killing of lay church workers, involving five people, in the south-eastern part of the country in 1982.

On 10 June 1982 Alfonso Galeano, a Catholic 'Delegate of the Word', of the Comarca of Las Pavas in the Municipality of Nuham, was killed by four men, three of whom were members of the militia. Galeano had been threatened several times before he was killed. The apparent motive of the assault was robbery, but Galeano was the only one of several people present who was killed. His assailants were detained but were set free soon afterwards.

Daniel Sierra Ocón, an active member of the Catholic Marriage Encounter movement, was detained under suspicion of contra activities. After being publicly presented on television and having confessed that his only crime was to have listened to *la radio clandestina* (one of the contra radio stations), he was set free. He was, however, required to return to prison to sign some papers. On 21 December 1982 his wife and family were informed that he had committed suicide in gaol.

Yamilet Sequeira de Lorio, supervisor for Catechism and Evangelisation in San Miguelito, Department of Río San Juan, Guillermo Lorio, her husband, and Juan Obando were arrested at dawn on Tuesday 19 July 1983. Neighbours said that the arresting officers arrived in a jeep of the DGSE (Directorate General of State Security). The corpses of the three victims were discovered later the same day, mutilated and burnt. The neighbours did not dare to touch them because of 'threats that were being made against them'. Finally, the remains were handed over to the family, who were obliged to bury them in haste.

Lenín Cerna, the head of DGSE, has stated that two of the cases were fully investigated and that those responsible were given 30-year sentences, and asked Bishop Vega to provide further information on the third case.[15] Aryeh Neier of Americas Watch also says that military officers have been tried and imprisoned for these crimes.[16]

The major item of evidence advanced to sustain the charge that the Sandinista government has systematically violated the right to life is the testimony of Alvaro Baldizón, who worked as a special investigator for the Ministry of the Interior with the rank of sub-lieutenant until he defected to the United States in July 1985. His accusations are contained in a document published by the US Department of State in February 1986 with the title *Inside the Sandinista Regime: A Special Investigator's Perspective*. Baldizón's personal testimony, however, has been found to be unreliable. It was analysed in detail by Americas Watch who found crucial contradictions about dates and places.[17]

Baldizón asserts that the Sandinista government has murdered 2,000 people in a systematic programme of extermination directed personally by Tomás Borge, Minister of the Interior. Human rights violations, however, are not difficult to investigate in Nicaragua and it is inconceivable that this number of people could have been murdered without reports being made to human rights organisations. Americas Watch estimates that the number of recorded killings outside combat and disappearances for which the Nicaraguan government is responsible in the last six years is 'close to 300'.[18]

Baldizón's personal unreliability does not necessarily extend to the documents which he brought with him when he defected. They were prepared by other officers and give every appearance of being genuine. These documents do not, as Baldizón and the State Department allege, indicate that the Nicaraguan government carried out a programme of special measures (executions) against opponents. The use of the phrase 'special measures' (*medidas especiales*) in one report shows that it was an official, or at least generally understood, term within the Ministry of the Interior. This report, written by Lieutenant Raúl Castro Gonzalez, contains the remark: 'It must be pointed out there is a list of counter-revolutionaries with whom special measures were taken and it is known to the most senior officers.' This key sentence is mistranslated by the State Department to read: 'I must point out that there exists a list of counter-revolutionaries with whom special measures were taken *with the knowledge of the superior officers.*'[19]

It is probable that the term was used as euphemism for summary execution. Seven named individuals and three unidentified persons, from a list of 31 people about whom information was sought, appear with initials 'm.e.' beside their names. Four of them are identified in the report as contras or contra collaborators. The other people on the list appear with the dates of their detention, initials of the arresting body (EPS — army, SE — State Security) and the supposed date of their release or transfer to the prison system (SPN). It is impossible to vouch for the accuracy of this or the other reports, but they appear to be conscientious investigations of abuses committed by government forces. Indeed, the investigation into the Puerto Cabezas killings and disappearances calls for stricter action by the Auditoría Militar (military prosecutor's office) against soldiers who commit abuses. In another document, dated 20 March 1984, an investigating officer reported that Sub-Lieutenant Ríos Torres had raped a Miskito woman in Lapán. In November 1984, eight months before Baldizón's defection, Americas Watch reported that Ríos Torres had been sentenced to 18 years' imprisonment for this crime.[20]

It is difficult to provide accurate quantitative figures for abuses carried out by government security forces or the army. Between 1982 and 1985, however, Amnesty International, Americas Watch and the Washington Office on Latin America documented 130 civilian deaths, in at least 22 separate incidents, including the 86 Miskitos mentioned above. Two of the incidents, causing 11 deaths, were the result of indiscriminate attacks by army patrols in a war situation. Four of the incidents involved drunken soldiers or militiamen. In ten of the incidents, there was an investigation by the government and in at least six cases those responsible were found guilty and sentenced to long terms of imprisonment. Owing to the patchy nature of the investigations conducted by the human rights organisations, these figures are inevitably an under-estimate of culpable deaths caused by government troops and security forces in that three-year period.

Nevertheless, given the continual monitoring of human rights abuses in Nicaragua by local organisations and international bodies, it is extremely unlikely that other major incidents, such as massacres, have gone unreported. Similarly, a large number of small incidents do come to light, if only as unconfirmed reports.

Over 600 Sandinista soldiers are at present serving prison sentences. According to the military prosecutor's office, the majority of them were found guilty of common crimes, such as robbery or assault. A small proportion, however, were found guilty of abuses of power. According to the prosecutor's office, one of its officers is attached to every active unit and is empowered to impose punishments in the field. In addition, every soldier carries a small manual, *El Manual del Soldado Sandinista*, enjoining good behaviour and encouraging him to report abuses of power or indiscipline to his officers. As noted above, the crimes committed by Sub-Lieutenant Ríos Torres came to light because they were reported by subordinates.

During the same period, the contras have been responsible for at least 1,185 civilian deaths.[21] Given gaps in the data and lack of knowledge about the fate of the hundreds of *campesinos* who have been abducted and forcibly recruited by the contras, this figure seriously under-estimates the number of civilians they have killed. The contras have singled out individuals for torture and execution because they are known supporters of, or work for, the government. They have been guilty of indiscriminate attacks on the civilian population, causing heavy loss of life.

Amnesty International and Americas Watch continue to call for a full and public explanation of past government abuses. Americas Watch urges the government to set up a reliable system for the prompt reporting of arrests to the families of those concerned. Both organisations confirm, however, that there is no government policy of extra-judicial execution or murder. Even allegations made by the CPDH do not suggest that extra-judicial executions or disappearances are sanctioned by the Nicaraguan government. The CPDH published complaints of 15 disappearances which occurred in 1985 and 16 deaths reported in 1985. These complaints, however, are published without further investigation. Only one or two of the alleged disappearances and four of the alleged murders by government troops or security forces in 1985 appear to deserve extensive further investigation.

The 15 'disappearances' reported by CPDH as occurring in 1985 include two cases where prisoners had been transferred from their prisons, one case where the authorities acknowledged having detained the individual concerned but where the relatives had not yet been able to see him, one arrest for a common crime, and two cases in which people had been inducted into the armed forces. In six further cases complaints were made to the CPDH between seven and 15 days after the arrest; in two cases, more than two months had elapsed. In all the cases except the prisoner transfers, the arrests were made in remote areas of the country. In the cases of the deaths Americas Watch reports: 'CPDH provided Americas Watch with copies of the complaints on the 16 deaths that had been reported to it since the beginning of 1985. Twelve involved individuals; one case involved four victims. One of these cases reportedly took place in 1983 in the course of a search of a house that led to a 'ninety minute shoot-out'. In another case the complainants report a capture and, apparently, the subsequent disappearance of that individual, not a killing. In four cases deaths are attributed to agents of the security forces but the causes are not related to political activities (e.g. a drunken agent firing into a dance hall; other cases involve personal enmities). Five cases involve combat with the contras; the relatives complain that the army took their children to fight unprepared, or did not give them enough information.

In the other four cases, there is evidence that the victims were arrested by security forces, presumably for investigation of contra activity. Subsequently their bodies were found. In two of these cases, witnesses reported to CPDH that the hands of the victims were bound and that they had been tortured.[22]

4. Torture

Few cases of physical torture have been reported to human rights organisations. Again, Amnesty International and Americas Watch state that there is no evidence that the use of torture is sanctioned by the Nicaraguan authorities. People detained for interrogation under the state of emergency regulations, however, have reported the use of conditions of detention and interrogation techniques which could be described as psychological torture. Other observers have referred to these interrogation techniques as 'white torture' (*tortura blanca*). Most cases of such interrogation techniques are connected with the DGSE detention centre of El Chipote in Managua.

Detainees report that the cells in El Chipote are below ground level and are ventilated only by a vertical shaft in the ceiling. The door is a solid metal sheet and has a small window flap through which the guards can inspect the prisoner. The light is switched on only for meals, otherwise the prisoner is kept in gloom, if not total darkness. Prisoners are issued with standard prison overalls, a pair of rubber sandals, soap, toothbrush and toothpaste. The lavatory is a hole in the floor at one end of the cell. Washing water is supplied by a pipe jutting out from the wall at head height above the hole in the floor. The water is turned on for about ten minutes a day. The cell also contains a bunk bed with a mattress.

The two ex-detainees interviewed form part of the 'civic opposition'. They are determined opponents of the government but insist that they have no contacts with the contras. Roger Guevara Mena is a lawyer who was asked by the Archdiocese of Managua to represent Father Amado Peña, a priest accused by the government of aiding the contras. Two video tapes were key pieces of government evidence. One showed Peña apparently discussing sabotage plans with a contra conspirator. In the second video Peña is seen to hand over a briefcase to a man waiting in a car; on being challenged by security officials, the suitcase is opened and is shown to contain explosives. Those who have seen both videos claim that the first is more convincing and that in the second Peña could easily have been the victim of deception. Guevara demanded that the government submit the tapes to independent scrutiny before allowing it as evidence. The government refused to do so. Peña was duly convicted by the *Tribunales Populares Antisomocistas* but was pardoned shortly afterwards. Guevara was not allowed to examine evidence against Peña. As a result of his energetic defence of Peña, Guevara was detained by the DGSE, interrogated for nine hours and kept in a cell at El Chipote. He was told after his detention that his wife, who was seven months pregnant at the time, had had a miscarriage and had been rushed to hospital, and that if he admitted to his contacts with the contras then he would be released quickly and could go and see her.

The other ex-detainee, José Altamirano, is a member of the Social Democrat Party and associate general secretary of the independent trade union federation, the *Confederación de Trabajadores Nicaragüenses* (CTN). Altamirano was detained on 14 December 1985 and released on 8 February 1986 at the petition of former US President Jimmy Carter. During that time Altamirano was held at El Chipote and accused of being a member of the contras. He was interrogated for eight days in sessions lasting from 15 minutes to three hours. His family was threatened and he himself was told that he could spend the next 20 years as a prisoner. Altamirano says that during his detention he agreed to incriminate other union members in an alleged contra plot, known as Plan Alacrán, and spent three weeks learning a specially prepared statement word for word. At the press conference, however, Altamirano denied the charges. As a result he was punished with two weeks' detention in a darkened cell.

Other ex-detainees who have been interviewed by human rights organisations have reported similar treatment at El Chipote.[23] Similar cases have been reported by Amnesty International and Americas Watch. They have in common a rigorous detention regime combined with threats about imprisonment and misinformation about family members, the consequence of which is to induce a state of acute anxiety and feelings of helplessness. In some cases the apparent objective of the interrogators has been to persuade the prisoner to make a false confession which will discredit him and his organisation by linking it publicly with the contras and in others to persuade him to inform on the activities of members of his organisation. Arrangements are made for family members to visit detainees in a special visiting room at El Chipote. Such visits are supervised by a DGSE official. Altamirano reported that his wife was urged by DGSE officials to encourage him to cooperate so as to secure more lenient treatment for him.

Human rights organisations and the International Committee of the Red Cross (ICRC) have made repeated requests to be given access to prisoners held in DGSE detention centres, but the government has so far refused to permit such visits.

5. Detention

In normal circumstances Nicaraguan law allows the police to detain suspects for up to nine days before bringing charges against them. Under the state of emergency there is no limit to the time for which someone suspected of a political offence can be held for investigation by the DGSE. The numbers of suspects held under the state of emergency and the length of time for which they are held have been among the main concerns of human rights organisations.

Apart from the state of emergency regulations, however, there is a system of police courts, set up in 1980, which are empowered to impose sentences of up to two years for cattle rustling, certain drug offences and violations of certain consumer laws. The police courts have been politically abused and some opposition activists have been sentenced under them. The accused do not have the right to confront their accusers, call witnesses, or appeal to the ordinary court system.[24] The new constitution places all courts under the jurisdiction of the Supreme Court. The government has not, as in the case of the *Tribunales Populares Anti-Somocistas*, used the state of emergency to justify the continued functioning of these courts or to exempt them from Supreme Court supervision. Until the National Assembly brings in legislation to amend the decree-law which established the police courts, they will — if they continue to function — be unconstitutional.

Under the state of emergency which was in force before 15 October 1985, it was reported that 25% of detainees were charged or released within a month after their detention, a further 50% charged or released between one and three months after their arrest, and the remaining

25% held for longer than three months before being charged or released. The length of time for which detainees were held was not changed by the declaration of the new state of emergency on 15 October.[25]

By July 1986, however, it appeared that the large number of detentions made under state of emergency regulations had prolonged the period which detainees were spending in pre-trial custody. The Juridical and Human Rights Commission of CEPAD (*Comité Evangélico Pro-Ayuda al Desarrollo*) found in some cases which were brought to its attention that people had been held for as long as three months without being interrogated. The Ministry of the Interior admitted that it had a problem on its hands and gave two reasons for this situation, first that there were a great many detainees and that it did not have enough trained personnel to conduct the investigations, and, second, that at the time of the arrest, it did not have firm information about a case. CEPAD was able to use its good offices to obtain the release of 27 people from the community of Ojote (Region I) after four months' detention.

There are several estimates of the number of people held under state of emergency regulations, as opposed to those who have been sentenced for security-related offences by the *Tribunales Populares Anti-somocistas* and, between 1980 and 1983, by the ordinary courts. Such people can be divided into those who have been charged and are awaiting trial by the TPAs, who are held in the prisons of the national penitentiary system, and those who are under investigation by the DGSE.

In a press conference on 18 July 1986 Tomás Borge, the Minister of the Interior, said that 1,802 people were being held on charges linked to contra activity. Of these, 1,025 were awaiting trial.[26] In an interview in July 1986 the CPDH estimated that there were 2,000 detainees held without charges having been laid against them. In the same *Washington Post* report the CPDH is reported as saying that 2,000 people were being held in Managua alone. According to another estimate provided by the CPDH in April 1986, about 600 people were being held in the national penitentiary system pending trial or appeal hearings in the TPAs and a further 1,500 were being held for investigation in DGSE facilities. Since no independent visits to DGSE facilities are permitted, it is impossible to dispute these estimates with alternative sets of figures. There are indications, however, that the CPDH figures are exaggerated. According to independent sources on the Atlantic Coast, at the time when the CPDH was claiming that the DGSE was holding 100-150 detainees in Puerto Cabezas and 80-100 in Bluefields, there were only 15 people in DGSE custody in Bluefields and none in Puerto Cabezas.[27] Americas Watch estimated in early 1986 that at any one time

300 or more prisoners were held in DGSE facilities. This number probably increased during 1986 as a result of the large number of detentions made by the security forces in an attempt to dismantle contra networks in the war zones.[28] This estimate is consistent with the figures released by the Ministry of the Interior in July 1986. Dr Vilma Núñez, the director of the CNPPDH, said in May 1987 that there were approximately 900 detainees awaiting trial for security-related offences in Managua and possibly 600 in the rest of the country. About 300 people, a figure which can fluctuate considerably, were held for investigation by the DGSE at any one time.[29]

6. Due process and trial procedures under the state of emergency

The major legal instrument used by the government against alleged political offenders is the Law for the Maintenance of Order and Public Security passed in July 1979 and modified in June 1982. The principal criticism of this law is that it relaxed the standards of evidence needed to secure a conviction and severely limited the time in which the defence could present its case. Since April 1983 all cases involving charges under Articles 1 and 2 of the Public Order Law have been heard by the *Tribunales Populares Antisomocistas* (Popular Anti-Somocista Tribunals — TPAs), a system of special courts similar to the special courts used to try former members of the National Guard.

Article 1 of the Public Order Law punishes crimes against national security such as submitting the nation to foreign domination, revealing political or national security secrets or secrets that threaten the economic integrity of the nation, damaging installations such as bridges for the purpose of weakening defence forces, bearing arms against the government, overthrowing local authorities, impeding the authorities from carrying out their duties, and conspiring to do the above. Article 2 proscribes sabotage and conducting attacks while wearing uniforms or using arms of war.[30] Several organisations expressed concern that these provisions could be used as a pretext to gaol dissidents on the grounds that the offences punishable under Article 1 are loosely defined.

Cases are tried by a lawyer, acting as president of the court, flanked by two lay judges who are drawn from the Sandinista support organisations known as the 'mass organisations'. The Ministry of Justice is responsible for appointing all three judges. There is a lower court and a higher, appeal court. At present there is only one *Tribunal Popular Antisomocista*, functioning in Managua, but provision exists for further courts to be set up in other parts of the country.

The Nicaraguan Supreme Court argued, as it had earlier argued against the setting up of the *Tribunales Especiales de Emergencia* to try former members of the National Guard, that all cases should be tried by the established court system under the jurisdiction of the Supreme Court. The then president of the Supreme Court, Dr Roberto Argüello argued:

> I do not like the name adopted by the tribunals calling themselves 'anti'. What we need in Nicaragua is a sole unity of jurisdiction and not one special proceeding over there and another one over there; we do not need diverse tribunals parallel to the unitary system of justice ..[31]

The IACHR state flatly, '. . . the People's Courts will be used almost exclusively to try persons accused of political dissidence.'[32]

In fact, after more than three years work by the TPAs, it is clear that the accusations made against defendants invariably link them with armed contra activity, as direct participants or as having assisted the contras in some way. In practice, therefore, the TPAs have defined the offences over which they have jurisdiction as those involving the use of violence against the government. If political dissidents who have not used or advocated or aided and abetted the use of violence have been tried by the TPAs, it is because they have been accused of offences involving violence. The responsibility for preparing these charges belongs to the DGSE, the state security service. In 1984, for instance, Americas Watch reported:

> Most of the hundreds of arrests which have taken place since the establishment of the state of emergency seem related to the violent activity displayed against the government by forces operating from outside Nicaragua and within the territory, with covert but undeniable support from the United States. When the detainees are charged, the charges are strictly related to violent activity. There have been no cases since 1982 where criminal accusations were overtly the vehicle to suppress free speech.[33]

The TPAs have been functioning since June 1983. In the period from June 1983 to May 1986 1,215 people were brought before them. The lower court sentenced 846 people to terms of imprisonment ranging from three to 30 years, and the appeal court reviewed 553 individual cases. Thirty-four defendants were acquitted by the lower court and a further 15 by the appeal court. According to figures provided by the TPAs, in addition to those who were acquitted, 126 defendants were set free during this period. Three cases were withdrawn, 72 defendants were amnestied and 41 sentences were quashed (*sentencia revocada*). Three defendants were pardoned (*indultados*), one was released by a measure described as *liquidación de condena* and six defendants received suspended sentences (*suspensión de ejecución de condena*). In addition, two defendants were given probation (*casa por cárcel*); three minors — under 17 years of age — were referred to the juvenile courts, and one defendant was transferred to the ordinary court system. The majority of those who were sentenced received sentences of between three and 10 years.

The TPA case files show that from the very start of proceedings there is a strong presumption of guilt. Many of the cases rely solely on the confession given to the Ministry of the Interior investigating officer by the defendant. The majority of the defendants are peasants from the war zones who are accused of collaborating with the contras, by providing them with food or information about the movement of local officials or army personnel.[34] Given the isolation in which such defendants live, it would be extremely difficult to make a strong case against them. Certainly, for the outsider reading the files, it is impossible to form a clear impression of their guilt or innocence. One Sandinista official excused the weakness of the prosecution case by claiming that to have given more explicit evidence would have revealed the source of government intelligence.

The judges of the TPAs are instructed to apply the rules of *sana crítica* (sound reasoning) in their evaluation of the evidence. Americas Watch states that this follows modern trends in Latin American law and that, 'As a result, courts are neither bound by strict rules as to the relative value of different types of evidence nor free simply to judge "in conscience". Courts must now find reasonable links between the evidence produced and the facts purportedly established by that evidence.'[35] The official definition of *sana crítica* is contained in Article 4 of the Law on Reforms in Criminal Procedure (Ley sobre Reformas en Materia Penal, Decreto 644 of 3 February 1981), which runs as follows:

> For the effects of this law, *sana crítica* is understood as the discretional appreciation of evidence of any kind, based on respect for the univocal standards of scientific, technical or artistic character, or of common experience; and in conformity with the fundamental principles of justice and sound reasoning. These rules and principles must serve as the basis for the reasoned decision of the court.

One academic lawyer in Managua stated that under the rules of *sana crítica* a confession unsupported by other evidence should not be sufficient to obtain a conviction.

In her summing up, however, one prosecution lawyer defined *sana crítica* as follows:

The search for the truth by way of the system of *sana crítica* must necessarily be situated in the social, economic, historical and political reality of our country. The litigants, like the Tribunal, form part of that reality and, for that reason, it is the common task of all, whatever their role in the trial, to contribute the elements of proof which will lead to the truth, moving away from the traditional conception of a trial as a contest between accuser and accused, as if only private interests were at stake. On the contrary, our participation in this trial should be infused with the public interest with which it is identical, the public interest being no more and no less than the supreme right of our people to defend itself.[36]

This case involved a group of *campesinos* from the mountains of Estelí who were accused of supplying the contras with food. If the argument of the prosecuting lawyer is taken to an extreme, the TPA system could be regarded as a quasi-judicial form of counter-insurgency, a way of removing from the war zones those *campesinos* whose loyalty to the government is dubious. In this case, it would be comparable with other measures taken by the government to protect and isolate the civilian population from the contras and allow the war to be prosecuted with energy, the most important of which is the resettlement of peasants from the war zones in different regions of the country.

Prosecution lawyers concentrated on the political aspects of the case, often making blanket denunciations of the contras, pointing out the the damage they do and the threat they represent, in order to persuade the judges to convict.

It should not be assumed, because of shortcomings in the procedures of the TPAs, that all the defendants are innocent. In some cases, such as those of the crew of a FDN plane shot down in 1983 and Eugene Hasenfus, the US citizen captured when a contra plane was shot down in October 1986, the defendants were evidently guilty of the offences with which they were charged. One defence lawyer, reviewing his cases, cheerfully admitted that in one case his clients had indeed been members of the internal front (*frente interno*) of the contras.[37]

Defence lawyers, for their part, differed on the best strategy for presenting a defence to the TPAs. One said that it was not productive to argue directly against the prosecution and that defence lawyers were more likely to obtain an acquittal or a reduced sentence if they dwelt on their clients' family circumstances, humble origins and so on. One lawyer, however, claimed that her client had been acquitted because she was able to prove that her client had been in custody at the time the offences of which he was accused had been committed.

The reading of court transcripts, however, gives the impression of a ritual rather than a legal defence. The defendants themselves routinely declared that they never signed the confessions of guilt produced in court and claimed that this, their court appearance, was the first occasion on which they had heard them. In two cases, they said they were asked to sign a document purportedly giving consent for transfer from one prison to another. Many of the defendants are illiterate, signing their alleged confessions with thumb-prints or extremely shaky signatures. It is fair to assume that they would be unable to read the type-written statements produced by the DGSE. It is commonplace, in ordinary criminal cases, for the defendant to allege at the beginning of a trial that any confession was extracted through torture or trickery. According to a lawyer working in a university legal aid centre, this is a habit that persists from the Somoza era.

One of the major difficulties for defence lawyers is the gathering of evidence to prove the innocence of their clients. The TPA regulations allow only two days for the defence to answer the charges and a further eight days, extendable to 12, for the presentation of evidence.[38] In practice, however, owing to the delays in the system, they are given much longer.[39] Nevertheless there are enormous difficulties in travelling to the defendants' home areas and gathering evidence. The only such evidence the author saw in a court transcript was a document signed by the defendant's neighbours attesting to his good character and innocence.

In July and August 1986 606 cases were sent to the TPAs by the DGSE. This represents a sharp increase over the previous rate at which cases were being processed. The Ministry of Justice is reported to have stated that the tribunals tried 160 people in the first five months of 1986.[40] According to one defence lawyer quoted in the same report, this increase is a response to the contra vote taken by the US Congress in June. It is more likely, however, that it reflects the Ministry of the Interior's known wish to reduce the growing backlog of detainees awaiting trial and the higher numbers of detentions during 1986. It is unlikely that the DGSE would have been able to prepare so many charges after 25 June 1986, when Congress finally approved the contra aid.

The composition of the TPAs, the lack of jurisdiction of the Supreme Court and the expedited trial procedures are all prejudicial to the due process of law. The Supreme Court has pressed repeatedly for jurisdiction over all courts of law in Nicaragua. The Nicaraguan government has justified the setting up of both the *Tribunales Especiales de Justicia* and the *Tribunales Populares Antisomocistas* by referring to the need for swift and exemplary justice. Relatives of people killed or maimed by the contras have complained about lenient treatment of contra prisoners and there is strong popular feeling against them. As mentioned above, some of the defendants are evidently guilty as charged, having been caught red-handed. In the other cases there is no way of telling from the court records what is the proportion of wrongful convictions. Certainly a number of defence lawyers were themselves convinced of the innocence of their clients. The system is clearly open to abuse. The defendants could be the victims of malicious accusations, grudges on the part of officials or simply excessive zeal. Until the government reforms the TPAs by demanding a higher standard of evidence and placing them under the jurisdiction of the Supreme Court, the suspicion must remain that they are used to remove from the war zones people who are suspected of aiding the contras or whose loyalty is merely in doubt.

In mitigation it can be said that, if this is the case, the TPAs are an extraordinarily laborious way of accomplishing this objective and also quite selective. If the TPAs do have a counter-insurgency objective then the number of people serving sentences imposed by the TPAs — 846 in three years — is small in relation to the extent of the areas in which the contras have operated. At the same time, it must be recognised that the government has a problem. The contras rely on information provided by local people to ascertain the whereabouts of army patrols and the travel plans of local government officials such as agricultural extension workers, health promotors and teachers. This information is used to plan ambushes. It is understandably a government priority to deny this information to the contras.

Although the new constitution places all courts under the jurisdiction of the Supreme Court, it will not have an immediate effect on the TPAs. The government has already announced that the TPAs will continue to function until the state of emergency can be lifted.

7. The prison system

When the Inter-American Commission on Human Rights visited Nicaragua in October 1980, its delegation inspected ten prisons in different parts of the country. With three exceptions — the Orlando Betancourt prison in Chinandega which was in the process of construction, the Ruth Rodríguez women's prison in Granada and the Francisco Meza youth rehabilitation centre — they found the conditions 'deplorable'. Overcrowding and poor food were the most frequent complaints. At the same time the delegation recognised that these conditions 'were due in large part to the special post war circumstances', and that 'of necessity the Government had to use the former regime's detention institutions, which the best of times had been rudimentary and which deteriorated notably in the years prior to the fall of Somoza.'[41] Between the time of the mission and the publication of the report, the government closed three of the prisons which had been most criticised by the IACHR. In its first report on Nicaragua in March 1982, Americas Watch also found severe overcrowding in the two principal prisons, the Cárcel Modelo Jorge Navarro (Tipitapa) and the Cárcel Héroes y Mártires de Nueva Guinea (Zona Franca) which were used to house 'Somocistas' who had been tried by the *Tribunales Especiales de Emergencia*.[42] IACHR reported some isolated cases of beatings of prisoners by guards but concluded that this was against government policy. The delegation was told that warders guilty of beating prisoners were themselves punished. Americas Watch 'encountered no credible reports of beatings or similar mistreatment at either Tipitapa or Zona Franca'.[43] Nevertheless other reports indicate that problems caused by brutal and authoritarian prison warders persist, although such behaviour is not condoned by the prison service.

The following account applies to the penitentiary system run by the government prison service. The detention centres run by the DGSE, where detainees suspected of security offences are held in pre-trial detention, are dealt with in section 5 above. There have been significant improvements in the national penitentiary service in the past four years. A system of farm prisons (*granjas abiertas*) was started in 1982. Now there are 14, 13 under the supervision of the prison service and one for soldiers who have been sentenced to terms of imprisonment by the military courts, which is under the responsibility of the *Fiscalía Militar*. A fifteenth open farm prison, for women, is to be opened shortly. Some of the farm prisons are classified as open and some as semi-open.

Tipitapa, Nicaragua's only high security prison, is no longer overcrowded. An Americas Watch representative who visited Tipitapa in March 1986 found it much improved and was told that it was operating at 80% of capacity.[44] Opportunities for work had been greatly expanded. 2,162 of Tipitapa's 2,860 inmates are former members of the National Guard or 'somocistas'.[45]

It is envisaged that the penal system in Nicaragua will offer the prisoner the possibility of a gradual progression through five stages to complete liberty on completion of sentence. The guidelines regarding the assignment of prisoners to each category of prison, however, are not in fact observed because sufficient open and semi-open prisons have yet to be built.

1. The first stage is the closed system, ordinary prison life without work.

2. In the second stage the prisoner is still held in a closed prison but is able to work and receives greater privileges and more visits. If the prisoner demonstrates good behaviour, he may, after serving 30% of

his sentence working in a closed prison, move on to the semi-open system. It appears that a prisoner may progress to Stage 2 as soon as he has been tried, depending on the availability of work in the prison to which he is sent.

3. In the semi-open system the prisoner is held in a low-security gaol with freedom to move around within the grounds, and is taken out to work during the day. After serving 20% of the sentence in the semi-open system, the prisoner moves on to the open system.

4. In the open system there are no security measures. The prison officials do not carry arms and the centre is run by an elected council of inmates. Contact with families is frequent. There are weekly visits; once a month the prisoner is given a weekend leave, and once every six months is allowed home for a week. After serving 10% of his sentence in the open system the prisoner is allowed home on probation.

5. During the probationary period the prisoner remains under police supervision but lives and works as a normal citizen. The penitentiary authorities are supposed to guarantee the probationer a job at this stage in his rehabilitation so that he will not be tempted to return to crime. It is not clear if they are able to do this in the present economic circumstances.[46]

Throughout the system, prisoners are encouraged to participate in cultural activities and to continue their education.

Since pardons are granted on the basis of good behaviour and evidence of rehabilitation, there is a strong expectation that once a prisoner has progressed to the open prison system his sentence will be drastically reduced by a pardon. There are evidently possibilities for shortening the stages outlined above because there are several former National Guard soldiers and officers, serving 20 to 30 year terms, who have already progressed to the open system. An evaluation of the open farm system, conducted between 1982 and 1984, found a very low rate of recidivism (15%) among participants. The psychologist who conducted the study found that '90% of the respondents indicated that their experience in the programme had helped them to see more clearly the forces at work in their lives and had in fact helped them to take more control over their lives.'[47]

The International Committee of the Red Cross (ICRC) is permitted access to all the prisons of the penitentiary system. In 1985 ICRC representatives started extended visits of three to four weeks, three or four times a year, to Tipitapa and Zona Franca. The detainees visited by the ICRC are former National Guard soldiers and 'Somocistas' and prisoners accused of, or sentenced for, counter-revolutionary activities. The ICRC is given unrestricted access to every part of the prisons and can talk to the detainees without the presence of witnesses. In September 1985 the ICRC reached an agreement with government permitting it to run seminars for members of the National Penitentiary Programme and the police.[48]

The only difficulty in the penitentiary system is with former members of the National Guard in Tipitapa, approximately 1,000 in number, who refuse to work. Americas Watch describes their prison regime as 'harsh'. They are limited to one family visit every two months. 'The system generates friction, as the prison authorities resent the inmates' lack of cooperation and refusal to accept the rules. Thus there are frequent breaches of discipline, and sanctions are imposed, including loss of visiting rights. Given the infrequency of visits, loss of entitlement to a single visit means that four months elapse between the times that they see their families.'[49] One person who has had contact with the 'non-cooperators' among the prisoners reports, however, that their morale is in general higher than that of those who do work, because they have a greater sense of their own worth, refusing to accept the premise of their gaolers that they need rehabilitation.

In a continent notorious for appalling prison conditions, where brutality and corruption are the norm, Nicaragua's penal system stands out as a genuine effort to find a more humane yet affordable alternative. Such criticism as there is concentrates on lack of resources, which is a feature of the Nicaraguan economy as a whole and is not limited to the prison system.

8. Population displacement

The displacement of people is part of war and Nicaragua is no exception. It is estimated that 250,000 people (8% of the total population) have been displaced within Nicaragua and a further 29,000 people are classified as refugees living outside the country. These figures do not include the contras nor the tens of thousands of Nicaraguans who have left the country voluntarily and taken up residence in the United States or neighbouring Central American countries for political or economic reasons.

The displaced in Nicaragua are peasants from the northern parts of the country and Miskitos and Sumus from the Atlantic Coast. The great majority of the displaced have moved voluntarily to escape the fighting and harassment by the contras. The most notorious case of involuntary displacement is that of the 8,500 Miskito indians who were moved from their communities along the Río Coco border with Honduras to the settlements of Tasba Pri. It should be noted here, however, that in 1985 these Miskito Indians were allowed to return to the Río Coco. This is discussed in Chapter 8. Over 50,000 peasants from the Pacific side of the country have been obliged to move by the government in the past two years. Some have been glad to move and others have done so against their will. As with other human rights issues in Nicaragua, the reality has been grossly distorted by the Reagan administration, which has claimed that the Nicaraguan government's resettlement programme is incarcerating peasants who do not support it in a 'Stalinist gulag'.

In 1985 the Nicaraguan government initiated a two-year plan for the resettlement of peasant families from the war zones of Region I (Estelí, Madriz and Nueva Segovia) and Region VI (Jinotega and Matagalpa). It is estimated that on completion 10,000 families (50,000) people will have been resettled in settlements (*asentamientos*). Many of those who have been moved were glad to move because their communities had already been attacked by the contras. Those who were members of cooperatives were particular targets. The 60 families at the Las Colinas settlement in Jinotega, for instance, are drawn from the Yali valley to the north of the town of Jinotega,[50] where 13 of the 14 cooperatives set up after the revolution have been destroyed in contra attacks.[51]

According to Americas Watch, in February 1986 approximately 55,000 peasants had been moved by the Nicaraguan government. Americas Watch representatives visited settlements in Nueva Segovia, Escambray and Nueva Aranjuéz, where they spoke to peasants who had been moved from farms in the north of Nueva Segovia.[52] Those they interviewed said that they had been given only 24 hours' notice of the move and had not been allowed to bring their animals, farm implements, household utensils or recently harvested crops. Other accounts confirm that the better-off peasants who were farming independently lost most and were most resentful at being moved against their will.[53] They did not feel endangered by military activity in the areas from which they had been moved and, in general, had not suffered at the hands of the contras. Much of the criticism voiced by these peasants concerned the way in which they had been moved. Their discontent was reflected in their refusal to join the militia or to cooperate in the defence of the settlement, which was, as they confirmed, entirely voluntary.

Other visitors to different settlements have reported that people felt safer there because, even when they had not themselves been directly threatened by the contras, they knew what they had done to others and were afraid of them.[54]

. . . Much taking of sides was strictly due to how contra or Sandinista combatants had conducted themselves in their hamlets. Most anti-government feeling was directed at the evacuation itself.
   A long conversation with people in [the settlement of] Estancia Cora who refused to participate in the defence of the settlement was

revealing: these people were attempting to maintain a strict non-involvement as a protection against reprisals by the 'contra'. And they were angry with the government because it had asked them to take up arms and compromise their 'neutrality'. I was struck by the fact that they were still very much afraid of the contra, who were no longer there, while simultaneously manifesting such little fear of the Sandinistas (who now presumably controlled their lives in the new settlement) as to complain indignantly to their face. They spoke freely to me of their decision and were determined to maintain their position. Whatever their complaints about the Sandinistas, fear wasn't one of them.[55]

The fact of resettlement has been softened by the government policy of dividing the land in the settlements and granting individual titles of plots of land to the resettled peasants. The size of the family plots varies according to a family's ability to work the land but the average size is 10 *manzanas* (7 hectares, 17.5 acres). The land is usually of better quality than the land which the family has abandoned. The settlements are better provided with health, education and extension services. They are usually sited on roads so that troops can be called in quickly in the event of attack. Some, at least, are relatively near the areas from which families have been moved, which gives them the possibility of visiting their original farms. The settlements, however, are themselves targets of contra attacks: between January and August 1985, 25 people were killed and seven wounded in contra attacks on five settlements in Region VI (Matagalpa-Jinotega).[56]

The settlement programme brings together a number of government priorities. It provides relative, if not absolute, security for members of cooperatives who, together with the government officials and promoters who serve them, are particular targets of contra attacks. It removes individual farmers from areas frequented by the contras in order to deny them the information and food on which they depend. It increases production since essential agricultural inputs can be provided more easily and facilities protected.

Another aim is to develop more positive attitudes towards the government among peasants who had previously been hostile or carefully neutral. The land grant scheme, positive discrimination in the distribution of foodstuffs and consumer goods, and the provision of housing and services are intended to accomplish this objective. Americas Watch reported that the peasants they interviewed remained deeply sceptical, almost a year after they were moved, and wanted to return home. Nevertheless, the programme does provide social services to peasants who, because of the war, cannot be reached by teachers and health workers.

9. Human rights organisations

There are three human rights committees in Nicaragua: the government-funded CNPPDH (National Commission for the Protection and Promotion of Human Rights), the Permanent Commission for Human Rights (CPDH) and the Legal Affairs and Human Rights Commission of CEPAD. The National Assembly also has a Human Rights Commission. The Moravian Church supports three legal offices under an organisation called the Association of Jurists of the Atlantic Coast, and the Law School of the Universidad Centroamericana (UCA) provides a legal aid service which assists in the defence of people charged under the Public Order Law.

The CPDH is openly critical of the government and has been accused by the government of publishing misleading reports. In November 1985 CPDH was told that it would have to submit copies of its reports for prior censorship. When Americas Watch representatives questioned Tomás Borge, the Minister of the Interior, about this later that month, they were told that there was no intention of censoring CPDH, but that the Ministry of the Interior wanted to receive copies of all CPDH reports as soon as they were published.[57] In May 1986, in what is considered to be a further positive step, the Ministry of the Interior began to answer CPDH's letters requesting information about individuals reported as detained.

CPDH's potentially valuable advocacy for human rights as a private organisation is flawed by its willingness to publish unsubstantiated allegations as fact. Its independence has also been compromised by donations from sources close to the US government:

The National Endowment for Democracy, a public foundation which distributes funds of the US government gave a concession of $50,000 for assistance in the translation and distribution outside Nicaragua of the Permanent Commission's monthly reports. The concession was administered by PRODEMCA, a group dedicated to Central American affairs. During the Congress debate in March over the package of $110 million PRODEMCA published full page adverts in the Washington Post and New York Times supporting military aid to the contras.[58]

In June 1980 the government set up the CNPPDH, thus implementing the recommendations made by a UN Human Rights seminar in 1978 regarding the setting up of national institutions for the protection and promotion of human rights, which were subsequently adopted by the General Assembly. Though government-funded, the CNPPDH is officially autonomous. In practice, the willingness of the CNPPDH to challenge the government has depended on the strength of character of its directors, of whom there have been several. As explained in Chapter 5, ii, one of the first tasks of the CNPPDH was to make recommendations for the pardon of somocista prisoners condemned by the Special Emergency Tribunals. Its conscientious performance of this task did not make it popular among Sandinista supporters who felt that imprisoned members of the National Guard and others fully deserved their lengthy prison sentences. Other tasks have included drawing up recommendations for prisoners to be released on probation and reviewing prison conditions. More recently the CNPPDH has devoted considerable effort to documenting contra abuses.

Although it is not part of CNPPDH's work to intervene on behalf of people detained for political reasons, its office, which is a short walk from the CPDH, is visited by many of the people who go to the CPDH to report the detention or possible disappearance of a relative because their primary concern is to obtain information and the person's release. There are some indications that CNPPDH under its new director, the former Supreme Court justice Vilma Núñez, will be more vigorous in investigating suspected cases of government abuse of human rights. Dr Núñez was responsible for a significant amendment to the state of emergency now in force. She persuaded the National Assembly to insist that the families of detainees should be informed by the DGSE of their place of detention. On 10 December 1986, Human Rights Day, Dr Núñez delivered a speech before President Daniel Ortega, Tomás Borge and the most senior officials of the Ministry of the Interior and Supreme Court. She said that the CNPPDH

> would carry out our investigations and promulgate our findings and ask for action by the competent authorities. Our commitment is to guarantee human rights to our people. Our difficult work must be part of the revolution, [part of] the respect for human rights. Besides fighting against the contras, it is also our job to fight for human rights. There are those who consider this policy idealistic in war time and costly to the revolution. But confronting them is the great majority of the Nicaraguan people who feel that it is necessary to defend human rights as part of the revolution.[59]

Not all the CNPPDH directors have spoken so directly or enjoyed the confidence of the authorities. Indeed, the last director but one, Mateo Guerrero, left the country and is now reported to be working with the contras.

CEPAD's Legal Affairs and Human Rights Commission was set up in 1985 to meet several needs. First, to advise Protestant denominations or churches which had no legal status (*personería jurídica*) and wanted to put their affairs in order. Second, CEPAD's member churches wanted a specialised commission to study the new constitution which was then being drafted and to make recommendations when it was submitted for discussion. Third, recognising that some abuses were being committed in the war zones by government soldiers, they wanted a commission which could gather, study and report on human rights violations. The commission has made representations to the government on behalf of members of Protestant churches detained under the state of emergency regulations and, in a number of cases, has obtained their release.[60] This success has brought extra work. Catholic priests are now bringing to CEPAD the cases of their own parishioners who are in detention.

The Human Rights Commission of the National Assembly is one of the Assembly's 12 specialised commissions. Originally its function was to report to the Assembly on bills relating to human rights and to make recommendations on pardons under the *Ley de Gracia* proposed by the CNPPDH. At the end of May 1986, the Commission approved 308 pardons (*indultos*) for persons including five Costa Ricans, five Hondurans and 60 contras, from about 580 requests. Three hundred further pardons were announced at the end of January 1987, including that of Sam Hall, the US citizen accused of spying whom the government judged to be unbalanced. The predominant criterion used to determine who should be pardoned is whether it is thought that those pardoned will not commit further crimes or, as some have, go over to the contras.

This commission is now taking a much wider view of its responsibilities. Its members have visited the war zones and the prisons and have interviewed high-ranking officials in the police and the prison system. As a result of growing concern about the large numbers of people detained under the state of emergency since October 1985, commission members had a meeting with Tomás Borge and Lenín Cerna, head of State Security (DGSE), on 28 July 1986. The agenda for this meeting included questions about the number of people who had spent more than two months in detention without being interrogated. The commission also wanted to discuss the possibility of opening trials of military personnel to observers. This concern arose following two suicides of military prisoners after they had been convicted in courts martial. In July 1986 an opposition member of the commission said he thought that its four FSLN members, out of a total of six members, were genuinely concerned with human rights. After the promulgation of the new constitution, membership was expanded to include members of the seven parties represented in the National Assembly.

The existence of these organisations, with their different functions and degrees of independence from government, is encouraging. They do not in themselves constitute guarantees for human rights but their experience shows that the government is willing to allow independent organisations to challenge the decisions of officials and to act on reports of abuses, especially when complaints are made by organisations which are not seen as politically motivated.

10. Day-to-day life under the state of emergency

Dwelling exclusively on human rights violations committed by the government or the contras can give a partial view of life in Nicaragua. In spite of the war and the state of emergency, Nicaragua does not give the impression of being a repressive society. There is a large resident foreign press corps. Journalists and delegations make frequent visits and are able to obtain and conduct interviews with private citizens and members of the opposition without government interference. Opposition politicians visit and receive frequent visits from diplomats based in Managua. There is no curfew under the state of emergency and, with the exception of the war zones, there is no restriction on movement around the country. Foreign tourists, including US citizens, are admitted to the country without visas. There is a considerable number of foreigners living and working in Nicaragua, of whom US citizens are the largest national group.

Everywhere the visitor will find young men and women in olive-green fatigues, some are soldiers on guard duty armed with AK-47 automatic rifles, others are off-duty or are members of the militia. They are almost invariably friendly even when they are refusing a request. Indeed, it is a frequent complaint of journalists that officials tend to prefer a misleading but gracious explanation to a simple refusal. The Sandinista police are famous for their courtesy and good manners and for being no respecters of rank when it comes to giving traffic tickets. One US resident has commented, 'If the police behaved here as they do in New York, we would be horrified.'

On Sundays Catholics go to the mass of their choice, celebrated by a priest in sympathy with, or hostile to, the revolution. Protestants, who have increased in number since 1979, go freely to their own churches, many of them simple chapels set up without official registration. Discotheques in Managua are open late into the night and, despite prices which are far beyond the ordinary Nicaraguan pocket, are full. They attract their share of 'internacionalistas' of course, but still the majority of the clientele is Nicaraguan. The ability of some Nicaraguans to eat and drink in expensive bars and restaurants is the consequence of the 'informal' economy, government incentives to producers of export crops giving them a proportion of their earnings in dollars, and the black market. Many Nicaraguans, like other Central Americans, receive remittances from abroad. They are able to change these dollars at the official 'parallel' or tourist rate of 2,500 córdobas to the dollar (February 1987) without having to identify themselves or give an explanation of how they came by the money. At that time the extensive black market was paying more than 3,000 córdobas to the dollar.

Dr Gustavo Parajón, the president of CEPAD, commented about the state of emergency:

> Despite the fact that in October 1985, when the state of emergency was imposed, we were alarmed and worried, life in general has not changed very much. There are restrictions on the political parties which need permission to hold their outdoor rallies. But for the common person there has been no perceptible change. The same restrictions apply for outdoor religious meetings but, in most cases, permission has been granted. As far as the work of CEPAD . . . is concerned, we have continued to operate as usual, and this is the case for other church and private organisations.[61]

6. Basic Economic and Social Rights

In 1978 and 1979 Nicaragua's GNP per head fell by one-third. At the same time Nicaragua, in common with the other countries of Central America, was facing a world which was sliding into recession. For Central America, and for developing countries in general, this meant high interest rates, lower prices for their major exports and relatively higher prices for essential imports. In addition, because of Nicaragua's contra war as well as the insurgencies in Guatemala and El Salvador and chronic trade imbalances between the more industrialised countries of Central America (Costa Rica and Guatemala) and their neighbours, the Central American Common Market, which had contributed significantly to economic growth in the 1970s, had virtually ceased to operate.

The 1979 insurrection in Nicaragua and the guerrilla wars in El Salvador and Guatemala were the product of, among other things, economic structures which systematically denied the most basic needs of the majority of the population. The FSLN and its allies in the Nicaraguan revolutionary movement made the satisfaction of those needs a priority, promising a dramatic restructuring of existing economic flows. The immediate inheritance of the war of insurrection was a serious economic crisis:

> Gross Domestic Product . . . fell by one third, industry had been bombed and looted, crops had not been sown for the 1979-1980 harvests, cattle had been slaughtered, airplanes and ships stolen, wages left unpaid, hospitals destroyed and foreign debtors unpaid. The cost of the war was estimated by the United Nations to exceed 1 billion dollars, in an economy with a national income of little more than double that figure. Somoza had run up an external debt of US$1.6 billion in the previous few years, but there was little evidence of productive investments. The funds had been used to

finance capital flight, and only US$3 million were left in the reserves from these loans and the bumper 1978-79 export harvest of cotton, coffee and sugar.[1]

Given the limited means at the disposal of the new government, it was inevitable that a restructuring of the economy would create 'winners' and 'losers'. Even if conflict about economic priorities was predictable, however, it was cushioned and dissipated by the national agreement that the assets of Somoza and his close associates, accounting for some 20% of all Nicaraguan productive assets, agricultural and industrial, should be expropriated. This satisfied the immediate political requirement to redistribute land and more than absorbed the management capabilities of the new government.

Nevertheless, the business sectors which had formed part of the political opposition to Somoza expected that their economic prominence would be reflected in terms of political influence after the insurrection. The open conflicts which surfaced in 1980 between the FSLN and the economic and political groups which had formed the *Frente Amplio Opositora* during the final year of struggle against Somoza were essentially a political dispute about the division of power in the new state. The resignation from the five-member junta of Alfonso Robelo was caused by the enlargement of the 33-member Council of State to 51 members. This measure, taken to give representation to new organisations that did not exist at the time of the insurrection, gave the FSLN a more secure majority. Subsequent political conflicts have been developments of this same theme, complicated since 1981 by the emergence of the contras as an externally financed insurgent force. Since then the opposition, both within and outside the country, has repeatedly criticised the economic policies of the Sandinista government. For an opposition which has sought through all the means at its disposal to portray the Sandinista government as illegitimate, the purpose of such criticism is more to fuel its political campaign than to win economic measures favouring private producers. The government has made numerous concessions to private producers, but these have been achieved by negotiations with producer associations rather than as a result of public debate about economic policy.

On taking power in July 1979 the new government nationalised the banks and foreign trade and adopted strict controls over the distribution of basic necessities. Within the limits imposed by economic crisis and simple underdevelopment, these measures enabled the FSLN to pursue an economic strategy which was designed to make an immediate positive impact on the income and welfare of the poor. Emphasis was placed on the provision of basic food needs, welfare, education, transportation and the provision of basic health services, which the Sandinista economists defined as the 'social wage'. They opted to remove these goods and services from the market in an attempt to deter speculation and avoid inflation.

The relative success of these policies in the initial years of the revolution, until 1983, when problems caused by the war came to dominate the economy, brought significant positive changes for the majority of Nicaraguans. This success, in contrast with the experience of the Somoza years, makes it possible to describe the Sandinista government as putting into practice a policy of basic economic rights. The negative consequences of this policy were felt by the rich and the middle class, who had been used to a stable and freely convertible currency which made US manufactured products available in Nicaragua for all who had the money to pay for them. After 1979 government control of the banks and foreign trade meant that permission was required for such imports.

Popular participation was an essential ingredient of the government's early successes. The achievements in education and health would not have been possible without the voluntary participation of thousands of Nicaraguans because the country simply did not have the resources to provide education and health care as services wholly provided and funded by government. The political significance of this participation was just as important as its practical contribution. For the first time ordinary Nicaraguans felt that they were assuming a degree of control over their own lives, that the state and its agencies could be responsive to their needs as they defined them and that they were significant both as individuals and members of communities. Now that the war has undermined some of the practical achievements of the early years, the sense of personal worth continues to motivate people who, if their political loyalty depended simply on a material accounting of the benefits or disadvantages of the revolution, should now be members of the opposition.

The first and most lasting achievements of the new government were in education. Its best known campaign was the National Literacy Crusade which mobilised 40,000 secondary school students between March and July 1980. As a result, the rate of literacy in Nicaragua rose from 50% to 87%. The literacy crusade was followed by an enormous effort in both formal and informal education. Between 1979 and 1984 spending on education increased by 450%. The number of children in primary education grew from 369,640 to 635,637; the number of secondary school students increased from 98,874 to 186,104, and of university students from 23,791 to 41,237. By 1984 there were 194,800 adults enrolled in courses, organised in study groups known as education collectives, covering the primary syllabus for the *campesinos* and workers who had learned to read and write during the literacy crusade. To accommodate this vastly increased school population, 1,404 schools and 48 higher education institutions have been built, with a total of 3,763 classrooms. Since 1979 the number of teachers has doubled, in the primary sector from 9,986 to 17,969 and in the secondary from 2,760 to 6,014.[2]

Improvements in health care have been equally significant. Before the revolution infant mortality was between 120 and 140 per thousand; polio, tetanus, measles, whooping cough and malaria, all of which can be controlled by relatively simple public health measures, were among the most common causes of death. Life expectancy was 52.9 years. In early 1981 vaccination and inoculation campaigns, together with massive programmes to control malaria-carrying mosquitoes and to distribute anti-malarial drugs, brought these diseases under control.[3] Since then the priority for the government has been the training of paramedical personnel, the construction of health centres and hospitals, the creation of mother's milk banks and centres for oral rehydration, which have helped significantly to reduce the number of deaths caused by infant diarrhoea. In 1984, according to Nicaraguan government statistics, 309 new health centres had been built, 5 new hospitals and 290 oral rehydration units were functioning, and 336 advanced technicians, 1161 health aides, 600 nurses, 550 doctors and 135 specialists were being trained. 350 of Nicaragua's 2,000 doctors left the country at the time of the revolution but the new generation of qualified doctors has more than filled the gap whichs they left. By 1983 the infant mortality rate had been reduced to 75 per 1,000 and 11% of the national budget was being spent on health care, as opposed to 3% before the revolution.

The successive phases of the land reform which began immediately after the revolution have changed the quality of rural life. In the 1970s, according to the 1970 census, the 1,700 families with large farms (over 350 hectares), constituting 0.9% of the total number of farming families, owned 1,622,000 hectares, 41.2% of the total cultivated land area. At the other extreme, there were 60,000 families with no land at all, 32.7% of the rural population.[4] The Nicaraguan countryside was organised to meet the needs of these large producers who needed an ample supply of cheap, seasonal labour to tend and harvest the cotton, sugar and coffee plantations. Following the expropriation of Somoza's assets, some of the largest farms in the country, with an area of 1,222,681 hectares (1,746,688 manzanas), 25% of all cultivated land, were transferred to the state (92.6%) and to cooperatives (7.4%), leaving the rest of the private sector virtually untouched, including 98,638 hectares (1,409,121 manzanas) in private farms of over 350 hectares.[5] The agrarian reform law was introduced to enable the state to redistribute idle or badly farmed land to peasant farmers, and then only for areas greater than 350 hectares. In 1980 peasant farmers who already owned land or who had to rent land from landlords benefited from controls on rents, which brought them down by 89% from the going market rate at the time, and from credit from the National Development Bank at 7% interest at a time when inflation was fluctuating between 35% and 80% per annum. It is estimated that 97,000 of the 110,000 *campesino* families received this concessionary credit in 1980.[6] This extremely generous policy was justified subsequently as necessary to reactivate production and assure an adequate supply of basic grains.

Subsequent amendments of the agrarian reform law, the latest in January 1986, have emphasised the role of private farmer and cooperatives in agricultural production, as opposed to the state sector. Three main reasons have been advanced for this change in emphasis: first, productivity in the state sector has been disappointing despite, or perhaps because of, substantial investment in intensive mechanised farming. Large state farms using modern technology have been adversely affected by the US trade embargo and shortage of spare parts caused by the lack of foreign exchange. Second, individual farmers, especially in war zones, are a less tempting target for the contras. Finally, some small farmers prefer individual titles since they offer a more tangible attachment to the land than the benefits of cooperative membership or employment on a state farm, and are more likely to support the government that has granted them. By the end of 1986, according to government statistics, 97,000 families, some 500,000 people in all (if it is assumed that the average *campesino* family has between three and four children as well as both parents), had benefited from the agrarian reform. In the north of the country and in the Atlantic Coast area the majority of the beneficiaries received *titulaciones especiales*, meaning that the state legalised squatters' (*precaristas*) rights.[7] The government intends to distribute land to a further 16,000 families in 1987.[8]

Both the intention behind these reforms and innovations and their execution in practice demonstrate that the Nicaraguan government was serious about making basic needs a priority. This is not to say that the government cannot be criticised for inefficiency, whether from inadequate management, bureaucracy or simple lack of foresight, the familiar faults of reforming governments. Both the Ministry of Health and MIDINRA, the agriculture and agrarian reform ministry, have been criticised on these grounds. These faults, however, have not been so serious as to overwhelm the reform programmes and their implementation, and the record up to 1983 shows genuine achievement. The success of the FSLN in the elections in 1984 was in part at least a popular vote of confidence in these policies, even though by then the toll of war had begun to undermine and even reverse some of the gains, especially in rural health and agricultural production and incomes.

The effect of the recession has also limited the ability of the government to expand welfare benefits. Fitzgerald maintains that the combined effect of low export prices and high import prices accounts for Nicaragua's chronic balance of payments deficit of US$400 million, because export and import volumes have remained stable.[9] The economic embargo imposed by the US government in May 1985 has exacerbated these difficulties because Nicaragua, in seeking to circumvent the embargo, has been forced to pay higher prices for essential imports, especially spare parts for plant and machinery which were already in use in Nicaragua before the revolution.

In spite of the effects of the war, the balance in terms of health and education is still positive. In 1986, according to Ministry of Health figures, the rate of infant mortality is 68.5 per 1,000 live births (1979 — 155), and life expectancy is 62 years (1979 — 56 years).[10] In some of the more remote, war-affected areas, however, doctors are complaining that they are once more seeing cases of third degree malnutrition after five years during which they saw very few cases. Infectious diseases, such as measles, have also reappeared because health workers can no longer visit areas where the contras are active (see above, pp.42-43).

The government has tried consistently to enlarge and extend these basic human rights to those sections of the population which did not enjoy them at all or could do so only precariously. Despite the privations imposed by the war, the record is still positive. In singling out schools, clinics and new agricultural facilities as targets, the contras are perceived by the Nicaraguan population, especially those most affected, as attacking human rights.

7. Civil Liberties

1. Freedom of expression

The issue of freedom of expression is particularly controversial. The war, as most foreign observers agree, justifies some degree of censorship. Nonetheless, Nicaragua, as the government from time to time acknowledges, and the opposition demands, needs a critical press. The Sandinistas maintain that they wish to uphold pluralism, and there is a political opposition which, within the four walls of the National Assembly, in interviews and small political gatherings, speaks out vigorously against government policies. The debate is important for Nicaragua but at the same time it is one of the issues which has been most used by interested third parties, such as the Reagan administration, to attack the Sandinistas.

The case of La Prensa

The arguments about freedom of expression have centred on *La Prensa*, the opposition paper which was suspended indefinitely by the government on 26 June 1986, following the approval by the US House of Representatives of the Reagan administration's US $100 million aid package for the contras. Until June 1986 *La Prensa* had been published after extensive censorship by the government Directorate of Communication Media (*Dirección de Medios de Comunicación*), a section of the Ministry of the Interior.

La Prensa was an opposition paper under the Somoza dictatorship. It was owned and managed by the Chamorro family, synonymous with the Nicaraguan Conservative Party, which has four presidents among its ancestors. Pedro Joaquín Chamorro became editor in 1952, but his early career was primarily as a political activist and conspirator against the Somoza dictatorship. In 1974 Chamorro took the major part of the Conservative Party into UDEL (*Unión Democrática de Liberación*), a more determined opposition coalition than had previously existed among the traditional opposition parties. In the 1960s and 1970s Chamorro made *La Prensa* a vigorous opposition paper which used all the resources of the written word, including ridicule, muck-raking and slanted stories, to attack the Somoza family. For much of this time *La Prensa* was censored or otherwise put under pressure by the Somoza government. In September 1977 Somoza was forced by the Carter administration to lift the state of siege then in force and to end censorship, thus freeing *La Prensa* to renew its attacks against the dictatorship. Chamorro's venomous attacks on Somoza cost him his life. He was assassinated on 10 January 1978. His attackers were never traced directly to Somoza but the government's handling of the case had all the signs of a cover-up.[1]

Under Pedro Joaquín Chamorro's sons *La Prensa* redoubled its attacks against the Somoza regime and became an overt supporter of The Twelve and the Broad Opposition Front until the insurrection. The personality of Pedro Joaquín Chamorro, who had been feted in the United States as a courageous opposition journalist, and the role played by *La Prensa* in the final years of the dictatorship, made it a symbol of press freedom. *La Prensa* inherited this mantle when it transformed itself into an anti-Sandinista paper in May 1980 and began to use against the new government all the journalistic devices which had been so effective against Somoza. This transformation was the result of a bitter political quarrel among the Chamorro family. The murdered Pedro Joaquín was replaced as editor by his brother Xavier, who wanted *La Prensa* to support the Sandinistas, but he was outvoted by other members of the family, Violeta de Chamorro (Pedro Joaquín's widow), Pedro Joaquín (his eldest son), Jaime Chamorro Cardenal (another brother) and Pablo Antonio Cuadra (a business partner). The quarrel was resolved when Xavier accepted 25 per cent of the assets of the paper which, together with the majority of the technical and editorial staff, he used to found a new daily paper, *El Nuevo Diario*, which supports the Sandinista government. Carlos Chamorro, another son, became editor of *Barricada*, the official newspaper of the FSLN.[2]

La Prensa became an anti-Sandinista paper after the resignation of Alfonso Robelo and Violeta de Chamorro from the governing junta in April 1980 but was published without prior censorship until the declaration of the state of emergency in March 1982. The paper was, however, closed on five occasions for one or two days.[3] The government took these measures under Decrees 511, 512 and 513, promulgated in September 1980, which provided for the temporary suspension of a news medium for wrongful publication of information that compromised national security or alarmist or misleading economic information.[4] One of these suspensions illustrates the sensitivities of the Sandinistas regarding the press. In July 1981 *La Prensa*, in discussing what would be a suitable wedding present for the government of Nicaragua to give to Prince Charles and Lady Diana Spencer, suggested a specially bound copy of the works of Carlos Fonseca, the founder of the FSLN, to send them to sleep at night. This was too much for the Sandinistas and was rewarded with suspension.

Between March 1982 and June 1986 *La Prensa* was heavily censored. Well aware of its capacity for scoring points against the government by letting people read between the lines, the censor regularly demanded extensive rewriting. On 20 February 1986 the censor refused to allow *La Prensa* to publish a news item about the expulsion of squatters from the university campus with the accompanying joke, 'Did you see that they've moved off all those people on the university campus? — Yes, I saw that, but I bet if it had been private land they would have moved more people in instead.' Other items censored included the headline 'A CONSTITUTION TO SUIT THE SANDINISTAS', although the news story below it, about the criticism of the Democratic Conservative party regarding the draft constitution, was not cut.[5]

Censorship, together with other state of emergency measures, was relaxed during the pre-election period of August to November 1984. *La Prensa*, however, refused to publish advertisements of any of the parties competing in the election or those of the Electoral Council encouraging people to vote. Coverage of political parties was highly critical and selective. For instance, *La Prensa* ignored altogether the closing rally of the FSLN in Managua, which attracted between 250,000 and 300,000 people. Extensive coverage, which was sometimes censored, was given to the activities of the *Coordinadora Democrática*, a right-wing coalition headed by Arturo Cruz, which boycotted the elections and advocated abstention. *La Prensa* editorial staff told a visiting US delegation that the paper deliberately withheld news of the other parties and gave preference to the *Coordinadora* because *La Prensa* was part of the *Coordinadora*. According to the editor of *La Prensa*, between 30% and 40% of the copy was regularly censored, though this dropped to 10% to 20% in the three months leading up to the elections of 4 November 1984. The items most frequently censored dealt with opposition to military conscription.[6]

Despite censorship, *La Prensa* never appeared as anything but an opposition paper. During the election period, from mid-1984 until November, the pages of *La Prensa*, the other two daily papers and specially assigned spaces on radio and television were open to the opposition parties. After the November elections the government maintained the relative tolerance extended to *La Prensa* in the pre-election period. Americas Watch commented, 'In fact, what *La Prensa* was actually allowed to publish was the harshest criticism of its own government that could be read in any newspaper in Central America during 1985.[7] The imposition of a more restrictive state of emergency on 15 October 1985 increased censorship to the point where, according to *La Prensa*, 60% of the copy submitted was rejected by the censor.[8] Nevertheless, during June 1986 *La Prensa* published harsh opposition party criticism of the draft constitution which was being discussed in open forums (*cabildos abiertos*) before being submitted to the National Assembly. *La Prensa* also reported extensively on President Reagan's efforts to obtain aid for the contras. Indeed, the last issue of *La Prensa* before its closure went to press on the evening of Wednesday 25 June with the headline 'REAGAN GESTIONO HASTA EL FIN' ('Reagan lobbied right to the end'), but went on sale on Thursday morning when the result of the pro-contra vote in Congress was known.

Foreign news coverage was slanted towards US positions, presenting the US as a haven of democracy and human rights and the Soviet Union as incorrigibly repressive internally and a supporter of terrorism abroad.[9] *La Prensa* also omitted stories which reflected well on the government or badly on the contras, despite their obvious significance in simple news terms. On 20 February 1986, for instance, *La Prensa* did not run a story about the killing by contras of a Swiss agronomist and five Nicaraguan women on the grounds that it had already been covered by the other papers.[10] Despite censorship, *La Prensa* posted copies of censored texts on its gates and distributed them to foreign embassies and opposition leaders.

The contra aid vote of 25 June 1986 in the US House of Representatives was the event which triggered the government's decision to suspend *La Prensa*. Jaime Chamorro, however, had risked government reprisals against the paper in April 1986, when he wrote an article in the *Washington Post*, openly supporting President Reagan's request for aid to the contras: '. . . Those Nicaraguans who are fighting for democracy have the right to ask for help wherever they can get it', he wrote. Chamorro claimed that the real danger of the Sandinistas was that they '. . . could inspire, aid and arm, from Managua, insurgencies throughout Latin America, "movements of national liberation" that will convert the entire continent into an immense base of insurrection.'[11] *La Prensa* was saved on that occasion by the defeat of the contra aid bill. Announcing the decision to suspend *La Prensa* on 27 June 1986, Daniel Ortega cited the grant which the paper had received from the National Endowment for Democracy in the United States and accused *La Prensa* of 'having become an accomplice of the aggression which the Reagan administration is launching against Nicaragua.'[12]

In the end the continued publication of *La Prensa* seemed to be the result of a complex calculation of political advantage on the part both of the paper and the government. For *La Prensa* the daily ritual of submission of copy, censorship and the preparation of new copy could be used to embarrass the government in front of the many foreign delegations which visited its offices. Survival under these conditions, however restricted, still kept alive an anti-Sandinista daily paper. For the government, the continued existence of *La Prensa* was a demonstration, however weak, of commitment to a 'free' press. The indefinite suspension of *La Prensa* has not ended the debate about censorship. On 2 August 1986 Daniel Ortega, speaking in Chicago, said that the government would be prepared to let *La Prensa* reopen if it agreed to stay within the 'present legality'. The 'present legality' refers to the strict limits which the government at present imposes on news and opinion.

The censorship debate

Today the debate about freedom of the press concerns the restrictions that may be properly imposed by the government in the present circumstances of war. Americas Watch, for example, has taken the view that it is proper to censor news stories of a military nature but considers that opposition to the draft '. . . is [not] the sort of military information that can be an appropriate subject of censorship during a military emergency.'[13]

The Nicaraguan government takes the view that the war is a national war, a war of defence of national sovereignty, and that no news medium can be permitted to undermine the nation's capacity to wage such a war. Supporters of the Sandinistas cite in the government's favour the draconian restrictions on the press imposed by countries such as the United Kingdom during the second world war. Indeed, all the limitations placed on civil liberties are defended with similar arguments. 'Low intensity conflict', of which the contra war in and against Nicaragua is an example, has been defined by US military theorists as 'total war at the grass-roots level'.[14] For the proponents of the low intensity conflict, military warfare is only a component, and not even the most important component, of this total war. In a country which is the victim of such a conflict, the dividing line between military and non-military information is blurred. All that is left is the arbitrary criterion adopted by government, manifested in the day-to-day decisions of the censor, opposed by the equally arbitrary yardstick of what in the circumstances is 'reasonable' in the eyes of members of the opposition or outside observers. Both government and its critics refer to measures taken by other states to restrict press freedom at times of national emergency.

The government's definition of the war against the contras as a war in defence of national sovereignty means that its central task, the defence of the nation against the contras and the US government, cannot be discussed. The government has said that it is willing to negotiate directly with the US government as the controller and funder of the FDN forces, and on three separate occasions has offered to sign the Contadora Treaty, which would proscribe cross-border activity by insurgent forces. It has refused to negotiate directly with the contras. This option for the ending of the war cannot be openly canvassed. Still less can it be a focal point for political mobilisation. In April 1984 the Nicaraguan Catholic Bishops' Conference called for a national dialogue including 'those Nicaraguans who have taken up arms against the government' in a pastoral letter which was not published by any of the three daily papers. Such direct expressions of opposition to policies which the Sandinistas and some of the 'loyal' opposition see as national rather than partisan would not be a problem if the Sandinistas had the willing support of virtually the entire nation. In fact, there is a significant minority for whom the war itself and the ways in which it can be brought to an end are the most important political issue.

Although the war has dominated the debate about censorship, it is probable that even without the war censorship would still be an issue. Articles 20, 21 and 22 of the 'Statute of Rights and Guarantees of Nicaraguans', published on 21 August 1979, state that the rights of freedom of information and expression can be restricted in the interests of the national economy as well as for reasons such as safeguarding the impartiality of the judiciary, preventing crime and maintaining national security, and that all propaganda against peace is prohibited. However necessary in the immediate post-revolutionary conditions of Nicaragua in 1979, the use of the terms 'national economy' and 'propaganda against peace' to justify restrictions is far from clear. Captain Nelba Blandón, who was responsible for the Directorate of Communications Media until November 1986, told members of the National Assembly on 7 July 1986 that the provisional media law 'was not in accord with the reality of the country because it does not establish how local news media can be obliged to convert themselves into a "vehicle for the education of the people".'[15] The desire to educate which has been a feature of the Sandinista government since 1979 seems irrelevant to the drawing up of a new press law, and could provide a further justification for control over the media.

Before the declaration of the state of emergency in March 1982, there were a number of incidents which gave some grounds for concern about the government's attitude towards freedom of expression: the prosecution and subsequent sentencing in October 1981 of three leaders of COSEP for publishing a letter to the government alleging serious economic difficulties and the refusal of licences to two radios on the grounds that their aerials were not properly placed according to the zoning laws, when, it was alleged, their real offence in the eyes of the government had been to broadcast comments critical of it. These and other less significant incidents,[16] do not, however, give the impression of an irreversible decline in press freedom before the declaration of the state of emergency. Americas Watch's later comment, referring to the period between December 1984 and October 1985, that *La Prensa* was allowed to publish the harshest criticism about a government to be found in any newspaper in Central America, applies with even more force to the period between May 1980 and March 1982.

There have been a number of incidents involving the censorship or closing down of media owned by the Catholic Church. On 12 October 1985 the government seized the first issue of *Iglesia*, a periodical issued by the Catholic Archdiocese of Managua. The government claimed that *Iglesia* had not been registered as a periodical, which Fr Bismarck Carballo, the press secretary of the Archdiocese, admitted, saying that he had only started the formalities of registration. Notwithstanding the failure to register the publication, it was unlikely that the government would have permitted the free circulation of a periodical like *Iglesia*. The first issue carried a report on a raid by armed officers of the Ministry of the Interior on Radio Católica on 12 September, to silence the transmission of a mass celebrated in Boaco by Cardinal Obando, a complaint about a second order prohibiting the transmission of a mass, a letter from the bishops' conference complaining about government attacks on the church, the text of a speech made by the Pope in the Dominican Republic under the headline, 'Latin America resists atheist models', and three separate and inaccurate complaints, from Granada and Río San Juan, about seminarians being forced to do military service.

There has been less comment about radio broadcasts, even though radio is by far the most popular medium. It has been estimated that the combined circulation of all three national papers in 1984 was approximately 190,000 (*Barricada* — 90,000; *La Prensa* — 60,000; *El Nuevo Diario* — 40,000).[17] There are now 46 radio stations, 25 of which are privately owned.[18] Before the current state of emergency, none was subject to prior censorship, though any news programme breaking government guidelines would have incurred government sanctions. During the 1984 election campaign, all competing parties were given free time on radio and television.

Even under the present state of emergency, there is space for debate and criticism on radio and television, and several radio stations, including those controlled by the government (The Voice of Nicaragua) and the FSLN (Radio Sandino) have 'phone-in' programmes in which people can air their views to invited guests. The best known programme of this sort is the weekly *Cara al Pueblo* (Face the People) on television, in which some of the country's top leaders, including Daniel Ortega, have been subjected to very robust criticism. Radio Noticia, an independent station, is much more forthright in covering news than either *Barricada* or *Nuevo Diario*. In December 1986, for example, Radio Noticia reported on the rumour of a possible merger between the Socialist Party and the FSLN, something that neither *Barricada* or *El Nuevo Diario* reported or, in the view of opposition politicians, would have reported, however well-founded the rumour.

On 1 January 1986 the government closed down Radio Católica, which was also directed by Fr Bismarck Carballo, for failing to broadcast President Daniel Ortega's end-of-year speech. Carballo acknowledged the charge, pleading human error.

We make no judgment about whether, at this stage of the war, censorship in Nicaragua is 'reasonable' or not. It is possible to understand the government's suspicion of *La Prensa* without seeking to justify the type of censorship which was imposed on it before it was forced to close. It is regrettable, if understandable, that there was no national paper which could discuss important political issues critically without provoking the censor. Before *La Prensa* was closed, the various Nicaraguan national papers were like people hurling insults at each other from opposite ends of a village street. *La Prensa* was snide and venomous, carefully culling the international news for reports which would cast as unfavourable light as possible on governments which supported the Sandinistas, principally those of the Soviet bloc. *Barricada* and *El Nuevo Diario* veered between stodgy solemnity and high-pitched indignation, about President Reagan, the contras and other enemies of the FSLN. These are 'front-page' characterisations. There is some good reporting in both papers. *Barricada* from time to time carries excellent long articles from journalists accompanying troops in the war zones. *Barricada* also carries Associated Press reports on the United States and other parts of the world without comment. Now that *La Prensa* has been closed and the government is encouraging discussion of the constitution, *El Nuevo Diario* has taken over the role of publishing opposition party statements.

The debate has concentrated on the national press. Nicaraguans, however, did and do have access to other publications which discuss national issues in more reflective terms, the monthlies *Envío* and *Pensamiento Propio*, both sympathetic to the government, but prepared to be critical and to publish the critical opinions of others. The publications of the different opposition parties (*En Marcha* of the Conservative Party, *Acción* of the Social Democrat Party, the Communist Party *Avance*, and the Socialist Party *El Popular*) circulate freely. The PPSC (*Partido Popular Social Cristiano*) has its own bulletin and a 15-minute daily radio programme *Día a Día*. The latter was closed down nine times in 18 months by the government censor. One two-day closure was punishment for having read out part of the pastoral letter issued by the Catholic Bishops' Conference on 6 April 1986. The bulletin has never been censored.[19] Some of the opposition parties, including the PPSC, are now discussing setting up a new newspaper, first as a weekly, and later, if all goes well, as a daily. They are trying to obtain politically untainted resources from Europe to finance the new paper. They are hopeful that there is space in Nicaragua for a paper which avoids the mistakes of *La Prensa*, accepting money from and acting as a press agency for the US government.

2. Freedom of religion

Freedom of religion is a two-sided issue in Nicaragua. On the one hand, though touching on the government's treatment of all the Christian churches and their leaders, discussion has focused almost exclusively on its relations with the Roman Catholic hierarchy, led by Cardinal Archbishop Miguel Obando y Bravo. For the purposes of this section, the Catholic bishops are treated as a group, united behind their official shared positions vis à vis the government. There are differences of opinion among the bishops, however, and the government has from time to time sought without success to exploit them. It is not our purpose here to describe the dynamics of the relations between the government and the Catholic hierarchy or the sharp divisions within the church. These have been discussed elsewhere. This chapter rather reviews the most severe sanctions and measures taken against Catholic clergy by the government since 1979.

On the other hand, the way the contras treat Christians and their churches, priests and pastors is also part of the issue of freedom of religion.

The major complaint of Cardinal Obando y Bravo is that the voice of the church is censored by the government. He set out these arguments in an article entitled 'The Sandinistas have gagged and bound us' in the *Washington Post* in May 1986.[20] In this article the Cardinal refers specifically to the closing of Radio Católica, the seizing of the first issue of *Iglesia*, a periodical which was to be published by the Archdiocese of Managua, the confiscation of the press used to print it, and the subsequent removal by the censor of the pastoral letter issued by the bishops' conference in April 1986. On 29 June 1986 he told journalists at his Sunday mass that the closing of *La Prensa* 'had extinguished the last glimmer of press freedom in Nicaragua'.

Since 1980 Archbishop Obando y Bravo, who was made a cardinal in 1985, has used his considerable authority to oppose the government and has attempted to reverse specific policies. The military service law (*Servicio Militar Patriótico* — SMP) is the clearest example. In September 1983 the bishops' conference published a pastoral letter, which was printed in *Barricada* the following day, condemning the conscription law presented by the government in August to the Council of State. The pastoral letter denied the legitimacy of the Nicaraguan state and, accordingly, its right to enforce a national conscription law, claiming that it equated the defence of 'the sovereignty and independence of the fatherland' with that of the 'popular Sandinista revolution'. The law also stated that one of the purposes of the SMP was to 'encourage a sense of discipline and revolutionary morale among our youth'. On the basis of these two phrases, the letter concluded that simply not being a Sandinista supporter should be sufficient grounds for being released from the SMP as a conscientious objector. The letter accused the government of 'taking advantage of military discipline to "manipulate" people ideologically and subject them forcibly to a given ideology . . .'.[21] This has been the official position of the Catholic hierarchy since 1983.

As noted above, the seized edition of *Iglesia* contained three complaints about seminarians being made to do military service. There are, however, serious doubts about the authenticity of the seminarians in question. Although the military service law makes no exemptions on the grounds of occupation or conscientious objection, the government has routinely excused both Catholic and Protestant clergy, including seminarians, from military service. In the case of the Catholic church, a commission of bishops provides the government with an official list of seminarians to facilitate this process. None of the 11 young men who were the subject of the protests in *Iglesia* were included in any such list. Several were registered as high school students in Rivas. In the event, five were allowed to return to their dioceses and six were retained for military service.[22]

Other pastoral letters in 1984 and 1986 have dealt with the theme of reconciliation, calling for dialogue with the contras. In 1986 the bishops, caricaturing the position of the government, said that, 'to opt for the annihilation of the enemy as the only way forward to peace is to opt inevitably for war'. Reconciliation has always been used by the cardinal to call for dialogue with, and recognition of the legitimacy of, the contras. Individual bishops, such as Mgr Pablo Antonio Vega, have gone further, stating that the government has forfeited its legitimacy to such an extent that the people have no recourse but armed rebellion.

These crucial political questions are the main point at issue between the Catholic bishops and the government.

This issue has been complicated by other incidents, some of which have gained the attention of the international media. The most important of these for church-state relations was the visit of the Pope to Nicaragua in March 1983. The failure of the Pope to address the issue of the war and the suffering it was causing provoked heckling at his open-air mass in Managua, and widened the rift between the hierarchy and the government, which had hoped that the Pope's visit would improve relations between them. Following the visit, the government took a harder stance towards the bishops, using its legal prerogatives to expel foreign clergy who were thought to be active opposition supporters.

The first such incident, however, took place in 1982. In August Fr Bismarck Carballo was paraded naked in the street of a Managua suburb after having been driven from a house allegedly by an enraged husband who found him in a compromising situation with his wife. It so happened that a camera crew was on hand to record the incident because, according to the government, it was covering a demonstration against a foreign embassy. Whatever the facts of the case — and to many people, including government supporters, it has all the features of a plan to discredit Fr Carballo — the crudity with which it was handled rebounded against the government.

Later that month a pro-Sandinista demonstration was fired on from a Salesian college in Masaya which had been occupied by some of its students in support of Father Carballo. One young man was killed and several injured. A Spanish priest, Fr José Morataya, was expelled after having been accused of complicity in this incident.

In May 1983 another Spanish priest, Fr Timoteo Merino, was expelled. He was accused of having used his influence in his parish in the south of the country to assist the ARDE contra group to develop its contacts among the rural population. On 31 October two more Spanish priests from the Salesian school in Masaya were deported, on the grounds that they had encouraged resistance to conscription, introduced in September, both verbally and with pamphlets. One of these priests, Fr Corral, denied vehemently that he had interfered in 'affairs of state'.[23]

In July 1984 Fr Amado Peña, a Managua priest well-known for his anti-government views, was arrested and charged under the Public Order Law, with having conspired with contras to commit acts of sabotage. The government evidence was two secretly filmed video-tapes, one showing Fr Peña allegedly handing a briefcase containing explosives to a contra agent, the other recording a conversation in which he apparently assented to contra sabotage plans put forward by someone who was ostensibly a member of the contra 'internal front'.

The charges were denied by Fr Peña, who claimed that he had been the unwitting victim of a government plot. Certainly the man who Peña thought was a contra conspirator was an *agent provocateur*. According to the defence lawyer appointed by the Archdiocese of Managua, the government would not allow independent experts to examine the videotapes. Fr Peña was tried and found guilty by the *Tribunales Populares Antisomocistas* but was kept under house arrest and amnestied in September 1984.

At the time of Fr Peña's arrest Archbishop Obando organised a protest march in his support. The state of emergency regulations stipulate that organisers of outdoor rallies or marches must obtain permission from the government. Archbishop Obando did not seek permission and, accordingly, the march was treated by the government as a deliberate challenge to its authority requiring a drastic response. The response took the form of the summary expulsion of ten foreign priests, only four of whom had taken part in the march. This measure, which removed some of the most effective conservative priests, was a clear warning by the government to the archbishop.

There were no further expulsions until 1986. On 29 June Fr Carballo was not allowed to return to the country after attending a meeting in Paris. Bishop Pablo Antonio Vega was expelled on 4 July. On a visit to Washington in March shortly before the first congressional vote rejecting aid to the contras, Bishop Vega had made statements about the situation in Nicaragua which had been used by President Reagan in his major speech in support of contra aid. In the wake of Congress' approval of the aid on 26 June and the judgment of the International Court of Justice against the United States two days later, Mgr Vega told a press conference that he thought the judgment was 'partial', that 'those to blame for a possible invasion would be those who have sustained themselves on support from one bloc alone' and that 'the aggression which we are suffering comes from an imperialism of the East'.[24] The significance in legal terms of the measures taken against Fr Carballo and Bishop Vega is that, even under the state of emergency, there is no legal statute which permits the government to expel a Nicaraguan citizen. Like other measures restricting civil liberties, they must be seen against the background of the contra war.

Contra attacks on church personnel

The contras have deliberately singled out for murder individuals thought to be supportive of the Sandinista government. In so doing, they have killed many people whose specific service to the community has been as catechists and 'delegates of the word' in the Roman Catholic Church and as pastors and lay preachers in the Protestant churches.

In 1984 a delegation of the National Council of Churches of Christ of the United States of America (NCCC-USA) reported that the Nazarene church had lost five churches in contra attacks, that four pastors of the Pentecostal Church (National Mission) had had to abandon their areas after threats were made by the contras, and that 20 congregations of the Assemblies of God in northern parts of the country had been disbanded as a result of contra activities. They also reported that three days before their visit the contras had machine-gunned a jeep belonging to CEPAD,[25] killing a woman and a six-month old infant. In 1983 a CEPAD nurse was kidnapped, raped and beheaded by a contra group.[26]

The contras have not murdered any Catholic priests or nuns although several priests working in the north and east of the country are said to have been marked down for assassination, and kidnapped and held temporarily. The worst atrocities have been committed against lay Catholic activists who support or have a role in government programmes. One of the most notorious cases is that of Felipe and Mery Barreda, both well known as Catholic activists in Estelí, who were kidnapped by a contra group on 28 December 1982 while picking coffee. They were taken to Honduras where they were tortured and killed outside a contra camp early in 1983.[27] Hundreds of lesser known Catholic activists have been killed by the contras since 1982. The targeting of church personnel continues. On 14 March 1986 at 11.40 p.m. a contra group operating in the Atlantic coast area burned down the Siuna house of the Misioneras de Cristo, a Catholic order of nuns. A young woman and four children were sleeping in the house at the time. The same contra group ambushed four cooperative members, shooting one and kidnapping two. One escaped. Subsequently the two who had been kidnapped also escaped and reported that this contra group had burned down the sisters' house because the Misioneras supported the revolution. They claimed to have a special group to deal with religious persons who got mixed up in politics and threatened that they were going to kill Sister Juanita Contreras. On 25 March the same contra group kidnapped a Delegate of the Word, Donato Mendoza, from his house. Two kilometres away they castrated him, gouged his eyes out, pulled out his fingernails, cut flesh from his legs, broke every bone in his body and shot him.[28]

On 31 July 1986 the contras killed three brothers, Nestor, Daniel and Filemón Castilblanco, all Catholics, who were working for the Baptist health organisation PROVADENIC in San José de las Mulas in Matagalpa. Jesús Barrera, a social worker with the Catholic church, was the fourth victim. This murder was carried out with the contras' customary brutality. The men were dragged from their homes in front of their families and tortured before they were killed. The body of

Daniel Castilblanco was found with one eye missing and Jesús Barrera had been castrated.[29]

Persecution, politics and subversion

The church hierarchy has itself taken measures against priests who support the government and is seen by Catholics sympathetic to the government as 'persecuting' that section of the church which is committed to social change and the defence of the revolution. Cardinal Obando has attempted to 'expel rebellious nuns and priests from the country or to transfer them to rural backwaters. At least 40 religious have had to leave the country, their congregations or the church because of such pressures.'[30]

In mid-1986, after six years of increasingly bitter exchanges, relations between the government and the Catholic hierarchy were similar to those between the government and *La Prensa*. The automatic presumption was of bad faith on both sides. The issue of military service illustrates the gulf that separates church and state. The fact that the hierarchy has been making political statements does not constitute a valid reason for censorship or control. In other Latin American countries the churches have played an important role in the defence of human rights by making political statements, and for that reason have been criticised by dictators for meddling in affairs that do not concern them. The dispute between the government and Cardinal Obando and Bishop Vega is their defence of the contras. Those who see the contras as legitimate actors in Nicaraguan politics will find no fault with this. The Nicaraguan government and a substantial number of Catholic priests and religious think that the contras, because of their barbarism and, more importantly, because they are armed rebels created and kept in existence by a foreign power, the United States, have no legitimacy. Those who share this view accept that Obando and Vega have stepped over the line between legitimate criticism and subversion.

The actions of the leading figures among the Catholic bishops, of the contras and of the government demonstrate that it is misleading to discuss the measures that have been taken by the government, or for that matter, the atrocities committed by the contras, in terms of freedom of religion. The NCCC-USA delegation concluded that it,

> . . . while recognising the serious problems in present church-state relations in Nicaragua due to the confrontation and tension between the government and the Catholic church hierarchy, finds no basis for the charge of systematic religious persecution; rather, it considers this issue to be a device being used to justify aggressive opposition to the present Nicaraguan government.[31]

This somewhat bleak view of church-state relations dates from mid-1986. Subsequently there have been improvements. As a result of the efforts of the new papal nuncio, Mgr Paolo Giglio, who arrived in Nicaragua in August 1986, dialogue between the Bishops' Conference and the government has been re-established. In November 1986 the bishops held a eucharistic congress in Managua without difficulty. According Mgr Bosco Vivas, the auxiliary bishop of Managua, the church-state conversations are being held in an atmosphere of 'frankness and goodwill'.[32]

3. Freedom of association

Freedom of association, like freedom of expression, is one of the most difficult issues in Nicaragua. If it is taken to mean freedom of association to organise opposition to the defence effort and the policies that flow from it, then there are severe and crippling restrictions. They affect in particular those opposition parties and unions which refused to take part in the elections, but also factions in the political parties represented in the National Assembly.

Trade unions

According to government figures at the end of 1983 there were 1,103 unions with 207,391 members. The FSLN-affiliated organisations had 167,111 members (CST — 111,498; ATC — 40,000; FETSALUD — 15,613). Other left-wing unions — CGTI, affiliated to the Socialist Party of Nicaragua, and CAUS, affiliated to the Communist Party of Nicaragua — had 17,177 and 1,939 members respectively. The CTN, aligned with the Social Christian party, and the CUS, aligned with the Social Democrat party, had 2,734 and 1,670 members respectively.[33] Both unions and their parties belonged to the *Coordinadora Democrática* which boycotted the 1984 elections.

All unions are affected by the suspension of the right to strike which has been in force since October 1982. The issue of freedom of association, however, affects mainly CTN and CUS. The government's membership statistics are disputed by CTN, which says that it is not possible for workers to affiliate openly for fear of victimisation. It is claimed, for instance, that 680 of Managua's 1,000 bus drivers are members of SIMOTUR, a CTN-affiliated union. Amnesty International and Americas Watch have described the harassment of CTN and CUS activists, including visits from Ministry of Interior officials to people's homes, requests to report to police stations, short-term detention and, in some cases, trial and sentencing by the *Tribunales Populares Antisomocistas* on charges of working with the contras. The effect even of a simple official visit to an individual's house can be sufficient to intimidate opposition activists, when they are ordinary union or party members without foreign or high-level political connections, and when they are only too well aware that under the State of Emergency regulations the DGSE is empowered to detain people indefinitely.

José Altamirano, associate General Secretary of the CTN, was held by the DGSE from 14 December 1985 to 8 February 1986, when he was released by the government in response to an express request by former US president Jimmy Carter. According to Altamirano, during the time of his detention he was repeatedly interrogated about his alleged contacts with the contras. His interrogators threatened to detain family members, saying that they could be held for up to 20 years. At one point during his detention, Altamirano agreed to testify against colleagues who had also been detained and spent three weeks learning his testimony by heart. At the press conference where he was to give this testimony, however, he refused to do so and was punished by 15 days in a darkened cell. Altamirano insists that his opposition to the Sandinistas is non-violent and denies that he is involved in any way with the contras. Other members of opposition parties state they have undergone similar experiences in El Chipote and that their interrogators' intention has been to persuade them to make a false public declaration of their involvement with the contras. The purpose of such confessions appears to be to discredit members of the right-wing opposition, particularly the *Coordinadora Democrática*, and their parties and unions, by identifying them with the contras, even when such an association cannot be proved.

The CTN has sent several complaints to the Committee on Freedom of Association of the International Labour Organisation (ILO). The complainants allege harassment and detention of non-Sandinista union activists, most of whom were members or leaders of unions affiliated to the CTN. The ILO's cumbersome official process of investigation has meant that in a number of cases the government has been able to reply that the detained CTN activists have already been released.[34] More frequently the government has replied that the trade unionists were arrested on the grounds of their participation in counter-revolutionary activity. Nevertheless, the ILO has expressed concern about the large number of members of workers' and employers' organisations who have been arrested.[35] Because of the delays in investigation, none of the cases discussed in these ILO reports is recent. Some insight into the issue of freedom of association is provided by Case 1185. One of the complaints referred to the sacking of eight bus-drivers who had allegedly been dismissed in 1983 from ENABUS on the grounds of their membership of the CTN. The Committee on the Freedom of Association noted 'with interest' that the General Labour Inspectorate had ordered their reinstatement,[36] an indication that CTN activists are harassed but that, at that time at least, there were some legal remedies available to them. There is no subsequent indication whether the legal order for reinstatement was in fact obeyed.

One unusual aspect of the complaints made against the Nicaraguan government is that Nicaraguan employers' organisations have, as they are entitled to do, also used the facilities of the ILO to lodge formal complaints. One such case (No. 1317) is the detailed and convincing evidence presented by Enrique Bolaños, chairman of COSEP, that in November 1984 a page was torn out of his passport at migration control at the airport in Managua so as to prevent him attending a seminar of representatives of Latin American employers' organisations which was to take place in Mexico.[37] As chairman of COSEP, Bolaños was, of course, a prominent member of the *Coordinadora Democrática* and an opponent of any accommodation with the Sandinista government.

Opposition parties

After the approval by the US Congress of the contra aid package in June 1986, there is very little space for opposition union groupings to organise. The most important issue for the government is defence, and it has made clear that any organisation which undermines its ability to mobilise resources and support for the war effort will not be tolerated. The situation has left opposition groups little option but to throw in their lot with the Sandinistas, moderate their opposition for the duration of the war or join the contras in the hope that they might win. The choice they make now will have a decisive effect on their political fortunes when Nicaragua returns to some sort of stable peace. Opposition parties represented in the National Assembly, however, continue to campaign against the government. At the end of January 1987 leaders of the PLI (Independent Liberal Party), Communist, Socialist and Popular Social Christian parties presented a writ to the Supreme Court challenging the legality of the state of emergency under the new constitution. Before handing in the document, about 100 party leaders marched through the streets of the capital.[38]

The legal opposition parties also report detention and harassment of party activists. The PLI, for example, protested that 50 activists in Mozonte and Ocotal were held for up to six weeks after being detained on 17 May 1986. Some party leaders, however, acknowledge that, because of the war, the DGSE may legitimately detain people for investigation. They do not think that it is too preposterous to suggest that one or two unwise party activists may have become involved in contra activity.[39] Cases reported by the PSC (*Partido Social Cristiano*) between October 1985 and April 1986 include two alleged murders by soldiers and DGSE officers and one alleged case of manslaughter. The most common complaint, occurring in 20 out of the 45 incidents published by the PSC, is that party activists had been intimidated or detained briefly for questioning. Representatives of the PLI, the Conservative Party and the PSC all claimed that party members were pressed by DGSE officers to inform on the contra activities of other members of the party.

The parties themselves are not banned and they are allowed by the state of emergency regulations to hold indoor meetings. They have to obtain permission to hold outdoor rallies. It appears to the outside observer that there is remarkably little for party members to do for their parties once the elections are over. At present, the parties do not have municipalities or local government authorities to run, and they cannot conduct public campaigns through the media in order to increase their membership. They seem to function as clubs and as networks of information for their leading figures, some of whom are members of the National Assembly. These networks will be reactivated when the next elections are announced. These are the municipal elections which are to be held in 1988.

Conclusion

The whole area of civil liberties is a problem in Nicaragua. The right to suspend the freedoms of expression and association at a time of emergency is recognised by international law. The extent and nature of the emergency which Nicaragua is facing has been described at length. It establishes a *prima facie* case for the state of emergency. One can acknowledge also that, in the context of this emergency, the DGSE performs a distasteful but necessary function, spying on people, gathering information, planting informers, infiltrating the opposition and, finally, detaining and interrogating suspects.

Despite the state of emergency, basic rights have been protected. Nevertheless, the state of emergency gives the DGSE very wide powers of arrest and detention. Use is made in interrogation of the threat of indefinite detention. At the same time, the ordinary citizen has no legal recourse against arbitrary detention by the DGSE. Although the experience of being detained, interrogated or threatened by the DGSE cannot rank with the crimes perpetrated by the contras, it is sufficient to instil fear in most ordinary people. The widespread use of these techniques and the large number of people who are released after questioning indicates that their purpose is to intimidate as well as to detect contra activity. Since these acts are primarily directed against known and open opponents of the government, identified by their membership of opposition political parties or unions, their effect may also deter people from lawful opposition.

This experience is not the same for all the opposition, falling harder on the more right-wing parties, which might be expected to be more sympathetic to the contras but nevertheless remain within the law. Mauricio Díaz, leader of the PPSC (*Partido Popular Social Cristiano*), a party that supports the broad aims of the revolution but is extremely critical of the FSLN, said in an interview (26 June 1986) about the state of emergency:

> There have been problems, but they've been resolved. Someone captured, someone detained, but nothing of greater significance. We have carried out effective action in the constitutional debate. We've had our own constitutional meetings. We're going to have one in Ocotal next Sunday. This Saturday our political commission meets to evaluate the situation, the approval of the $100 million. So I cannot say there has been systematic repression against us, at least. Evidently, there are other parties that have bigger problems with the government.[40]

8. The Atlantic Coast

1. The region and its history

The Atlantic Coast region covers almost half the land area of Nicaragua. It is heavily forested and extends from the central highlands across the coastal plain to the Caribbean. Its inshore waters are a rich fishing ground, especially for lobster and shrimp, and inland there are gold mines at Siuna, Bonanza and Rosita. Most of the valuable timber has already been extracted by companies which closed down in the 1950s. Two other companies ceased operations at the end of the 1930s. In 1981 the population of the Atlantic Coast was estimated at 282,000, divided as follows: *mestizos* 182,000, Miskitos 67,000, Creoles 26,000, Sumus 5,000, Caribs 1,500, Rama 650.[1] In 1980 the Atlantic Coast, with approximately 10% of the total population, contributed 4.7% of Nicaragua's gross domestic product.

The protagonists in the controversy about indigenous rights are the Miskito, Sumu and Rama peoples, but it also affects the *mestizos* and the Garífuna and Creole communities concentrated in and around Bluefields in the southern part of the territory. The long history of enmity between the Miskito and the Spanish-speaking *mestizos* of the Pacific side of the country is the background and substance of the present conflict. The Miskitos were witnesses to the extreme cruelty with which the Spanish settlers subjugated and annihilated the Amerindians of western Nicaragua. To this day they refer to white and *mestizo* Nicaraguans as 'Spanish'. British pirates established bases on the Atlantic Coast and subsequently it became official British policy to use the Miskitos to combat Spanish influence in the Caribbean and Central America. In the late 18th century, the British crowned one of the tribal chiefs King of Mosquitia. As US interest in the area grew, British influence waned in the 19th century and was formally brought to an end in 1860 by the Treaty of Managua which acknowledged Miskito rights by providing for the setting up of a 'reserve of Mosquitia' to perpetuate limited autonomy under the Miskito king. All this was brought to an end in 1894 when the government of José Santos Zelaya militarily occupied the Atlantic Coast, naming it the province of Zelaya, deposed the king and forced the Amerindian leaders to sign a declaration of allegiance to Nicaragua.

The Atlantic Coast was neglected under the Somoza dynasty. There was no road between the Pacific and Atlantic sides of the country. The Amerindians were largely left to their own devices in small rural communities where they spoke their own languages and worshipped in their own churches. The Moravian church, introduced by missionaries in the mid-19th century, is the major denomination among the Amerindians and is the region's major grass-roots institution. Sandino's forces were active in northern Zelaya from 1930 to 1933 but memories of him are mixed: he treated prisoners harshly — as did the other side — and his raids coincided, and became linked in some local inhabitants' memories, with the disastrous effects on the local plantation economy caused by the economic depression of the 1930s.

2. Conflict

The series of events leading up to the present conflict is clear. There was little military activity on the Atlantic Coast during the insurrection, which was viewed as an entirely 'Spanish' affair, and the Amerindians looked somewhat askance at the Sandinista activists who came to announce their liberation. The writer of a report for the Board of World Mission of the Moravian Church in the United States reported:

> The nationwide emphasis on literacy and health care, and on the institutionalisation of the revolution through mass organisations, was introduced on the Atlantic Coast by the Western Nicaraguan Sandinistas with enthusiasm, haste and good deal of insensitivity. In November 1979, government officials ordered the dissolution of ALPROMISU [Alliance for the Promotion of the Miskito and Sumu, founded in 1972 with the encouragement of local Moravian leaders and funded from abroad through CASIM, the Moravian development organisation and CEPAD, the Evangelical Committee for Developent Aid] and then, in the face of community protests, permitted its reorganisation as MISURASATA [Miskitos, Sumu, Rama and Sandinistas United]. Meanwhile the regional distribution of consumer goods, which had always been sporadic and precarious, suffered new blockages as a result of nationwide

economic dislocations; this further angered the east coast people, especially those who had money to spend.[2]

The charge of insensitivity has been admitted many times by the government. CIDCA, the government institute for research on the Atlantic Coast, commented:

Given the low standard of education in Nicaragua, and the difficulties of political organisation under Somoza, the demand for political cadres and professionals outstripped the numbers of such people available. In addition, one must take into account the language barrier, the different attitudes and roles of lower ranking church personnel in both regions and the lack of previous contact between the two coasts. As a result there was a high potential for cultural insensitivity, misunderstanding and lack of respect. If to this we add a strong component of mutual racial prejudice, the emergence of problems was almost a foregone conclusion. In such an atmosphere, any attitude which could be interpreted as a lack of respect, not to mention clear racial abuses, was attributed, not to the individual responsible but to the 'Spanish' in general and the Sandinista revolution in particular.[3]

Daniel Ortega attended the inaugural assembly of MISURASATA in November 1979 and it seemed that any breach had been healed. Steadman Fagoth, who was elected president of MISURASATA, became a member of the Council of State, and the organisation, like mass organisations in western Nicaragua, sought funds from the government and set about community organisation. The first clash on the Atlantic Coast, in fact, was with the Creoles, not the Miskitos. In October 1980 there was a three-day strike in Bluefields, and demonstrations against the presence of Cuban doctors, nurses and school teachers. Police were flown in from Managua and several hundred people were detained overnight. The leaders, however, members of the SICC (Southern Indigenous and Creole Community), were not released until September 1981. The Creoles have not subsequently opposed the government as a group but their attitude since has been described as lethargy or passive resistance.[4]

MISURASATA was treated as a mass organisation and given major responsibility in the organisation of the Literacy Crusade in the Amerindian languages. There was also a Literacy Crusade in English for the Creoles. One of the problems of working through an organisation with a primarily ethnic identity was that positive national achievements were constantly credited by the beneficiaries to MISURASATA rather than the FSLN and the government. To this day many Miskitos believe that the Literacy Crusade in their language was organised and paid for by MISURASATA.[5] Often government employees and FSLN activists were accepted by indigenous communities only when they could produce a letter of recommendation from MISURASATA.[6]

In February 1981 the government put Steadman Fagoth and 21 other leaders of MISURASATA in preventive detention. The charge of separatism had been levelled against MISURASATA by Sandinista officials on the Atlantic Coast for some time. MISURASATA had been put in charge of a project to draw up and formalise the claims of the Amerindians to land on the Atlantic Coast. The government was informed that Fagoth and Brooklyn Rivera, who had remained on the coast as the full-time organiser of MISURASATA, planned to use the closing ceremony of the indigenous language Literacy Crusade in Puerto Cabezas, to which the three members of Junta had been invited, to present a claim for 38% of the land area of Nicaragua in front of thousands of Miskitos.[7] Fagoth had been reported as telling a MISURASATA assembly that the 'Spanish' would need passports to visit the Atlantic Coast. Then, on 20 February, an arresting party of Sandinista soldiers tried to detain a Miskito literacy worker during a church service in Prinzapolka. Four Miskitos and four soldiers were killed. There were mass demonstrations of protest, and churches and offices were occupied. The Sandinista leadership reacted to this new form of civil disobedience first with uncertainty and then with repression.[8] There were more arrests, which prompted some 3,000 young Miskitos to flee to Honduras. All the MISURASATA leaders but Fagoth were released in an attempt to pacify the horrified Miskitos. While Fagoth was still in prison, the government made public a dossier showing that he had worked for Somoza's secret police. This made little impact on the Atlantic Coast. The most common reaction was one of suspicion. Fagoth was released in May on condition that he try to calm down the Amerindian communities and then leave the country for a while. Instead he went immediately to Honduras, where he joined forces with the remnants of Somoza's National Guard, who were already operating as a counter-revolutionary group and used the 15 de Septiembre radio to call for the 'liberation of Nicaragua from Sandino-communism'.

The two sides rapidly grew apart. Miskito demands for autonomy became more radical and the government became less inclined to make concessions. In their declaration of principles about the Atlantic Coast, the government declared 'Spanish is the official language of Nicaragua', but promised the indigenous communities '. . .the means necessary to develop and enhance their cultural traditions, including preservation of their languages.' It went on: 'The natural resources of our territory are the property of the Nicaraguan people represented by the Revolutionary State.' The government had decided to deal directly with individual indigenous communities. The FSLN, however, had lost all credibility on the Atlantic Coast and MISURASATA no longer existed. Towards the end of the year attacks from Honduras increased. The numbers of dead mounted, both of Sandinista soldiers and civilians collaborating with the government. Sixty people were said to have been killed in November and December 1981. The contra attacks were marked by extreme savagery. Torture, mutilation and rape were common. On 20 December near San Carlos 12 government soldiers were killed and a helicopter shot down.[9] According to Americas Watch, 'some seven soldiers were tortured, mutilated and killed'.[10]

This was the context of the Río Leimus incident. On 22 December 1981 35 Miskitos returning to their villages from Puerto Cabezas were arrested. The following night 17 of them were taken away by their captors and executed. In response to demands for an investigation first made by Americas Watch and then by the Inter-American Commission for Human Rights, the government carried out an investigation. Americas Watch was subsequently told that the soldiers responsible had been disciplined and were, in 1984, still serving prison sentences. CIDCA's *Trabil Nani* report, without mentioning this specific incident, also acknowledges that excesses were committed by Sandinista troops on the Atlantic Coast at this time.

Sandinista officials have acknowledged that there were problems of indiscipline and inexperience in the first year of the war. These were particularly acute on the Atlantic Coast, where young Spanish-speaking soldiers were treated virtually as an army of occupation by the local population, whose language they did not speak and whose culture they did not understand. CIDCA acknowledges that 'a certain number of indigenous communities in combat areas, particularly those in the north, have been the victims of abuses, brutal mistreatment and even criminal offences.'[11] At the same time, however, CIDCA points out that the majority of the human rights violations reported to its researchers occurred in the period July to September 1982, '. . . when the first important [contra] camps were discovered.'[12] CIDCA too points to the difficulties facing the Sandinista soldiers at that time:

. . . Many soldiers who were posted [to the Atlantic Coast] from the Pacific from August 1979 to the middle of 1982 came with prejudices and negative stereotypes. Of these, one of the most common was that the Miskitos were contras. If we add to that the inevitable tensions provoked by combat, ambushes and of living in a war zone, it is difficult to find the serene soldier who will distinguish between those Miskitos who are members of a [contra] task force, sympathisers, involuntary collaborators or villagers who simply want to get away from the fighting.[13]

The government announced that the insurgents had put into action a plan, code-named 'Red Christmas', to foment rebellion among the communities along the Río Coco — the river frontier between Nicaragua and Honduras — with the aim finally of capturing Puerto Cabezas, declaring it a 'liberated zone' and demanding international recognition. In response, in February 1982, the government took the very controversial decision to move the Miskito communities from the Río Coco to an area 50 miles south of the border. About 8,500 villagers were moved. Although there was no official advance notice of the move, word filtered out and some 10,000 Miskitos fled across the river to Honduras. The majority of the Miskitos who made the move to the four camps in the new settlement area, known collectively as Tasba Pri (Free Land), had to walk much of the way because there was no road. The communities of the Río Abajo area were transported by lorry and bus. The old, the very young, pregnant women and the sick, however, were airlifted in helicopters. The government made a considerable effort to ensure that the move was carried out without hardship. There was no deliberate cruelty on the part of the Sandinista forces. The greatest trauma for the Miskitos was the forced abandonment of their communities and the destruction of the villages, burning of crops and the killing of their animals carried out by the Sandinista forces to deny them to the insurgents. The motive for the move was military: to prevent the Miskito rebel groups from establishing a social base among the Río Coco communities and to facilitate military operations. The reasons advanced at the time by Sandinista officials, that the Tasba Pri communities would enable government agencies to bring the fruits of development to the Miskitos, in the form of better health care, housing, education and agriculture, while true up to a point, were rationalisations of what was seen as a military necessity.

The Tasba Pri camps were not, as has been alleged, concentration camps. In time, after the Miskitos had cleared the land and built the houses from materials provided by the government, they became settlements which, in their physical infrastructure, were superior in quality to average working-class *barrios* in the cities and peasant dwellings. The houses were close together, however, and set out in the straight lines and blocks, in the fashion of unimaginative planners the world over.

There were two further forced relocations of Amerindians after February 1982. In November 6,000 Miskitos and Sumus were moved to a makeshift camp at Wiwilí, near Jinotega, from the north central border with Honduras. Americas Watch comments that '. . . because of heavy fighting immediately preceding the evacuation, in the area near Raití, where these Indians lived, the need for evacuation was readily accepted by those relocated.'[14] Between July and September 1983 the inhabitants of ten small villages in northern Zelaya were moved when a contra force was operating in the area.[15]

Both Amnesty International and Americas Watch have reported that up to 72 people from the Puerto Cabezas area disappeared after being detained by security forces between July and October 1982. Americas Watch mentions 69 disappearances and Amnesty International 72, from a list compiled by the Moravian church in 1983, of which 44 cases are considered 'better-documented detentions'. Some dependents of those 'disappeared' have been granted government pensions, although they have not received from the government any formal statement acknowledging government responsibility for the fate of their relatives.[16]

3. A new approach

By 1983 it was becoming apparent to the Nicaraguan government that the militarisation of the Río Coco had not worked, even in military terms, because it had not prevented the Miskito contra organisation, MISURA, from setting up camps. Faced with the realisation that the increasing polarisation between FSLN authorities and the indigenous communities of the Atlantic Coast was creating the social base for the contras which it had sought to avoid, the government began to change its approach to the Atlantic Coast. On 1 December 1983 the government granted an amnesty to all those who had been convicted of criminal offences in northern Zelaya between 1 November 1981 and the date of the amnesty. Three hundred and seven prisoners, some serving long sentences, were released immediately. In December 48 Miskitos arrested in southern Zelaya were also released. By mid-1984 only eight Miskitos were still in prison. A new amnesty was announced in February 1985. In July 1986 the Moravian church reported that there were no Miskitos in prison for political offences.

This change of approach has been reflected in three separate but mutually dependent policy changes: (1) the setting up of organisations and procedures to discuss autonomy proposals for the Atlantic Coast; (2) the decision to undertake direct negotiations with the Miskito insurgent organisation MISURASATA, led by Brooklyn Rivera and allied with ARDE based in Costa Rica, direct negotiations being subsequently held in Nicaragua with local field commanders from both MISURASATA and MISURA, led by Steadman Fagoth and allied with the FDN based in Honduras; (3) the decision to permit and encourage the Miskito communities from the Río Coco to return to their villages along the river. This applied both to Miskitos who had fled to

Honduras in 1981 and to those who had been forcibly relocated to the Tasba Pri settlements.

This process was assisted by the creation in June 1984 of MISATAN, a Miskito organisation with a base of support among the communities of northern Zelaya, which argued that it was in the long-term interest of the Miskitos to negotiate and cooperate with the Sandinista government. MISATAN was led by Miskitos who were sympathetic to the Sandinistas, some indeed FSLN members, but was not a Sandinista organisation. MISATAN has clashed with the government on a number of important issues. It has had unpopular officials removed from responsibilities on the Atlantic Coast and has managed to persuade the government to abandon conscription of young Miskitos. In November 1985 MISATAN withdrew from the Regional Autonomy Commission of North Zelaya in protest at the government's inflexibility.

There were four separate rounds of negotiations between the government and Brooklyn Rivera, the leader of MISURASATA, between December 1984 and May 1985. The talks broke down at the last meeting with the government accusing Brooklyn Rivera of being inflexible and vice versa. The issue on which the talks broke down was the membership of an oversight commission to supervise peace talks. Brooklyn Rivera wanted a tripartite commission, with two members each from MISURASATA and the government, together with one representative each from the Organisation of American States, the Nicaraguan Catholic Bishops' Conference and the World Council of Indigenous Peoples. The government position was that this supervisory function should be fulfilled by people from the Atlantic Coast, mutually agreed by both sides. The government refrained from mentioning that two of the three groups proposed by Rivera had a record of hostility to the government.[18]

The possibility of a negotiated peace on the Atlantic Coast, however, had raised expectations among Miskitos in Nicaragua and Honduras, and the government and MISATAN were able to go on to negotiate a number of local peace agreements with individual commanders from both MISURA and MISURASATA. Throughout these negotiations the government demonstrated considerable flexibility. The Miskito insurgent groups which signed peace agreements with the Sandinistas were allowed to keep their arms and were given militia functions in the areas which they controlled. The Sandinistas even supplied them with ammunition. The response of MISURA was to try to reassert its control over its field commanders. In August 1985 MISURA was dissolved, Steadman Fagoth expelled and, with the active participation of US officials, a new organisation called KISAN was created under the leadership of Wycliff Diego, a Miskito loyal to the FDN and the UNO

(National Opposition Union), the coordinating body for all the contra groups receiving US aid. The following month, however, KISAN also split into two factions, 'pro-peace KISAN' and 'pro-war KISAN', with the pro-peace group signing local agreements with the Nicaraguan government.

The National Autonomy Commission was set up in December 1984. A regional autonomy commission for North Zelaya, with 39 members, was set up in January 1985, and the South Zelaya commission, with 27 members, the following month. The first document prepared by the commissions was published in July 1985 and was intended to serve as the basis for a process of consultation (*consulta*) with the communities of the Atlantic Coast. This document, which was published in Miskito, Sumu and English, as well as Spanish, opted for a concept of regional autonomy rather than national or ethnic autonomy; that is, it did not treat the Miskitos as a nation, as some of their would-be leaders such as Brooklyn Rivera would prefer, but as members of geographically defined communities within the patchwork of the Atlantic Coast. The document sets out in broad terms the rights of the Atlantic Coast people, including their cultural rights. It states that:

> The Popular Sandinista Revolution recognises that the indigenous peoples and communities of the Atlantic Coast have full rights to preserve and develop their own cultural traditions; to their religious and historical patrimony; to the free use and development of their languages; to be educated in their mother tongues and in the Spanish language; to organise their social and productive activities in accordance with their values and traditions. The culture and historical traditions of the indigenous peoples and communities of the Atlantic Coast form part of, and enrich, the national culture.[19]

The document also stated that the indigenous peoples and communities had the right to 'the use of the lands, forests, surface, underground and coastal waters of the areas where they live'.[20] The document includes the numbers of each population group, making clear that the majority of the people of the Atlantic Coast are the 120,000 *mestizos* (Spanish speakers of mixed blood), and that, although the Miskitos are the largest indigenous group (80,000), the other groups, Creoles (30,000), Sumus (8,000), Garifunas, also known as Caribs (1,500), and Ramas (800) have equal rights.

The return to the Río Coco started at the same time as the autonomy process. In January 1985, a group of 33 people returned to the village of Bismuna. In the course of 1985 15,000 people moved back, including the inhabitants of the Tasba Pri settlements. Many of the returning Miskitos took with them the corrugated zinc roofs of their Tasba Pri houses.

All these developments have been accompanied by fighting — near the mining towns of Bonanza, Siuna and Rosita which KISAN 'pro-war' forces have tried to capture and which are near the FDN infiltration routes to Boaco and Chontales, and by continued conflict in the south and central parts of the region where the FDN is active. The fighting, however, has not interrupted the talks with local 'pro-peace' commanders. At the same time the government has established a strong and permanent military presence throughout the Atlantic Coast which is preventing the Miskito contra forces from establishing the large and semi-permanent bases which they were developing in 1983.

It is a difficult process and there have been setbacks. In October 1985 KISAN 'pro-war' followers attacked and destroyed a strategic bridge at Sisín, the defence of which had been entrusted to a 'pro-peace' faction, thus creating enormous difficulties for the transport of supplies and equipment by the government and relief agencies to the newly resettled communities. In January 1986, after the bridge at Sisín had been repaired, KISAN began a campaign to persuade Miskitos living on the Río Coco to flee to Honduras. Several hundred KISAN fighters came over from Honduras. There were 30 attacks and ambushes of Sandinista troops in the first three months of 1986. This was accompanied by increased military activity by Honduran and US troops on the other side of the border. On 25 March the Sandinistas launched a counterattack against the KISAN camps, which were in or near several of the Río Coco villages. There was only one confirmed civilian death.[21] The fighting, which went on for several hours, gave rise to rumours about Sandinista atrocities. Many Miskitos crossed the border immediately to escape the fighting. In the following days many more were told to leave by KISAN. By mid-April approximately 12,000 Miskitos had again crossed the Río Coco into Honduras. In May and June, however, following the refusal of the United Nations High Commissioner for Refugees (UNHCR) to continue assisting refugees in the immediate vicinity of the river and an attempt by KISAN to make them move 50 kilometres further into Honduras, where they would be eligible to receive UNHCR assistance, several thousand returned to Nicaragua.

The attempt by KISAN to empty the Río Coco area of its traditional inhabitants seems to have had two purposes. The first was to provoke unfavourable publicity for the Sandinistas in the United States in advance of the congressional vote on contra aid. Americas Watch concluded that 'The arrival en masse of the refugees at reception centres of the UNHCR was carefully stage-managed so that it would coincide with the scheduled arrival of the journalists to be helicoptered in by the US Embassy.'[22] A plan was made to fly in some 60 journalists from Tegucigalpa but it had to be dropped because of high winds. The second purpose is less clear. Americas Watch has speculated that KISAN wanted to remove these Miskitos, indoctrinate them, and then, at some future date, make them go back again to form a more reliable social base. Certainly a large refugee population in Honduras would ensure a continuing flow of 'humanitarian' aid to the border area where KISAN has its bases, and provide a ready source of recruits for the contra forces. It is also speculated that this is consistent with a possible plan for a contra attempt to take and hold Puerto Cabezas as 'liberated' territory.

Despite these difficulties, the autonomy process has continued. In July 1986 a symposium was held in Managua to discuss the autonomy issue, attended by Miskito representatives including several 'KISAN pro-peace' leaders, the Moravian church, CEPAD, Tomás Borge and international participants. It had been planned that both the Regional Autonomy Commissions should present their drafts of an autonomy statute based on the consultation process started after the publication of *Principles and Policies for Autonomy* in July 1985. Because of the destruction of the bridge at Sisín and the renewed fighting in the north, the North Zelaya commission was unable to present its draft. In the south, however, where the truce with the Miskito insurgents held, the southern commission consulted 90% of the communities in the Bluefields area and produced its draft in time for the symposium.

The draft includes a detailed plan for a Regional Assembly which would be elected from ten zones, one of which is Bluefields. Each would have a minimum of two representatives and a maximum of four, except for Bluefields, which would have six. The purpose of assigning a minimum representation to each zone ensures that adequate representation is given to the less populated zones and to the smaller minorities.[23]

On defence, the draft specifies that:

> The defence of the communities and zones of the autonomous region rests primarily on the indigenous population and the ethnic communities of the Atlantic Coast, and this will be carried out in accordance with the framework of national defence policy and under the command of the Popular Sandinista Army.[24]

This appears to be an attempt to formalise the situation obtaining in the three zones where pilot autonomy projects were started in May 1986. The nine communities of the Yulu project zone, south-west of Puerto Cabezas, are defended by the 480 KISAN 'pro-peace' troops.

According to the Nicaraguan government, in the course of 1986 1,000 Atlantic Coast contras laid down their arms. Between March 1986 and March 1987 10,000 Miskito refugees are said to have returned to Nicaragua from Honduras.[25] The reduction in the fighting on the

Atlantic Coast has enabled government promoters to move about the region and to restart development and health programmes which were suspended because of the war. Considerable problems remain. In Zelaya Norte, 45,000 people, 50% of the population, are displaced, and many are dependent on supplies which have to be transported to the Atlantic Coast from the Pacific side of the country.

The past seven years have been traumatic for the indigenous peoples of the Atlantic Coast. The experience, first of Sandinista insensitivity and then of forced relocation, fighting and human rights violations, and then of coercion, cynicism and more human rights violations at the hands of forces commanded by men who claim to be champions of the Miskito people, has made them profoundly fearful and suspicious, almost as much of their own leaders as they are of the Sandinistas. The Miskito communities have fragmented, abandoning the vague but pervasive ethnic nationalism expounded by Steadman Fagoth in 1980. It is reported now that the Atlantic Coast communities are much more open to the idea of unity among all the inhabitants of the region.

The government, for its part, has responded pragmatically, abandoning its earlier facile and patronising attitude to the Atlantic Coast, which, in crude terms, blamed all the problems on the false consciousness of the local people derived from their long association with British and then US imperialism. They realise that they will be able to defend the Atlantic Coast against the contras only if they persevere with the peace and autonomy processes. This is a slow process. Even without a war it would be difficult to overcome the suspicions of the Miskito communities. As the hasty flight to Honduras in April 1986 showed, it is still relatively easy for the contras to disrupt the process, and one can reasonably assume that they will do everything they can to prevent the Nicaraguan government from developing popular support in an area which they regard as its Achilles' heel.

The autonomy process, however, is continuing. The North Zelaya Autonomy Commission presented its draft proposal in November and in early 1987 the two commissions met to draw up the joint proposal for presentation to an assembly of representatives from all over the Atlantic Coast which was held in Puerto Cabezas in April. Meanwhile more and more Miskitos are returning to Nicaragua from Honduras because they are no longer convinced by KISAN propaganda and, in many cases, because they have been press-ganged, threatened or physically abused by the contra forces. The MISURASATA fighters in the south have virtually abandoned the war. More fighters have given themselves up under the government's amnesty provisions and some Miskito contra groups have agreed to work as militia units for the government.

9. The New Constitution

Verdicts on Nicaragua's new constitution, promulgated on 9 January 1987, are already in: the new constitution is either a model of Marxist-Jeffersonian synthesis, designed to secure to the children of the Sandinista revolution the blessings of socialism and democracy, or a cheap public relations trick, intended to throw a hasty mask of liberalism over the brutal face of dictatorship.

The truth, as with any document written for the ages, will be in how it withstands the test of time. For the time being, all anyone can do is examine the genesis of the document, try to say in what ways it is like and in what ways unlike its predecessors and make some attempt to speculate about its future.

1. The constitutional process
The new Nicaraguan constitution may or may not 'work'. Whether it does or not, the process by which it was adopted has already added a new chapter to the political history of Latin America. Here is a country which, if not 'Marxist-Leninist', is certainly leftist, radical and revolutionary. Yet, unlike any other such country in this century, Nicaragua has chosen to draw up its constitution by a method both extraordinarily lengthy and uncommonly democratic, even by Western standards.

The constitutional process took two full years, from the assumption of office by the President and the National Assembly in January 1985 to January 1987, compared with the four-and-a-half months which the Aquino government in the Philippines devoted to a similar task.

On 29 April 1985, following several months of debate about such questions as whether the new constitution was to be a fundamental charter or a flexible instrument subject to continuing amendment and modification, and what role the opposition parties and the people at large were to play in its elaboration, the President of the National

Assembly appointed a Special Constitutional Commission consisting of 22 members. Although the FSLN had obtained 63% of the popular vote in the elections of November 1984, it took only 12 seats, or 55%, on the Commission, with three going to the Conservative Democratic Party (PCD), two each going to the Independent Liberal Party (PLI) and the Popular Social Christian Party (PPSC), and one each to the Nicaraguan Socialist Party (PSN), the Nicaraguan Communist Party (PC de N) and the Marxist Leninist Popular Action Movement (MAP-ML). The six-member Executive Committee of the Commission was equally divided between three FSLN representatives and one representative each from the PCD, PSN and PPSC.

By the end of 1985 the Commission had completed a process of consultation with parties, trade unions, and religious, cultural, professional and popular organisations in Nicaragua, and had sent delegations to 16 East and West European and Latin American countries to study their constitutions and their constitutional experience.

On 21 February 1986 the Commission released the first draft, consisting — in accordance with the Latin American tradition of detailed constitutions — of 221 articles divided into 32 chapters covering everything from fundamental principles to agrarian reform, forms of property and individual rights. By this time, consensus had been reached on certain basic guidelines:

- A quadripartite government (legislative, executive, judicial and electoral);
- Political pluralism;
- A mixed economy;
- Respect for democracy and individual rights;
- Recognition of the collective rights of the indigenous population, particularly those of the Atlantic Coast;
- Non-alignment and anti-imperialism.

Major difficulties remained, however, both between the various parties and within the ruling Sandinista party itself, on such questions as the definition of the family, the role of religion, which branch of government should be the ultimate arbiter of constitutionality, whether or not the armed forces should be called 'Sandinista', the extent of autonomy for the Atlantic Coast, whether the international law of human rights should be incorporated by reference, the procedure for declaring a national emergency and which constitutional guarantees may be suspended following such a declaration.

From 18 to 20 April 1986 a multi-party delegation of 23 Nicaraguans joined over 100 US constitutional scholars, lawyers and legal workers at New York University Law School to analyse and discuss the draft in a series of specialised workshops and plenary sessions. The sending of such a delegation, from a tiny country to a super-power dedicated to the violent overthrow of its government, is a tribute to the vigour of democracy in both countries.

After a period of intense preparation and several postponements, the draft constitution was submitted to the people of Nicaragua in a giant seminar conducted by means of 73 open forums, organised by sectors (women, teachers, journalists, Christians etc.), and held throughout the country from 18 May to 30 June. The discussions in the forums, which were attended by more than 100,000 people, filled more than 100 notebooks with points, resolutions and proposed amendments. They were greeted with suspicion by some of the opposition parties, fearing that they would be used by the FSLN to radicalise the constitution by appealing to 'popular demands'. The result, as will be seen, was almost precisely the opposite.

Discussion of the constitution, however, was not limited to the forums. Throughout the period of popular consultation, as well as before and after, contributions and criticism came from all quarters. Even the normally anti-Sandinista Catholic Bishops' Conference submitted a fairly conciliatory 'Pastoral Contribution'.

The scope of the demands put forward in the forums was enormous and contradictory: that God be named in the constitution; that Marxism-Leninism be so named; that abortion be prohibited, and that it be legalised; that wife-beating be made a constitutional offence; that greater safeguards for economic equality be provided; and that economic equality be eliminated as contrary to human nature.

Following the period of popular consultation, a second draft was submitted to the National Assembly, where it was debated in long, daily sessions, from 16 September to 19 November 1986. While there are interesting changes from the first to the second draft, the more significant amendments, representing the distillation of the national dialogue as well as the inter-party debate in the Assembly, are reflected in the final version promulgated on 9 January 1987. Some of these will be discussed below, with particular emphasis on the provisions dealing directly and indirectly with human rights.

2. The final version

The Nicaraguan constitution, in its final version, consists of a preamble and ten titles or sections, titled respectively, Fundamental Principles (I), The State (II), Nationality (III) The Rights, Duties and Guarantees of the People (IV), National Defence (V), The National Economy, Agrarian Reform and Public Finance (VI), Education and Culture (VII),

The Organisation of the State (VIII), Administrative Political Divisions (IX) and The Supremacy of the Constitution, its Reform and Constitutional Laws (X).

Title IV, which may broadly be defined as the human rights section, is by far the longest, accounting for one-third of all the articles (69 out of 202). It is divided into six chapters dealing with individual, political, social, family and labour rights and those of the communities of the Atlantic Coast. Students of constitutional economy might wonder at the length of this Title, in view of Article 46, which reads:

> In the national territory, each person is entitled to the protection of the state and to recognition of the rights inherent in the human person, to the unqualified respect, promotion and protection of human rights, and to the full effect of the rights defined in the Declaration of Human Rights; the American Declaration of the Rights and Duties of Man; the International Covenant on Economic, Social and Cultural Rights and International Covenant on Civil and Political Rights of the United Nations and the American Convention on Human Rights of the Organisation of American States.

This article is remarkable for three reasons: first, the Nicaraguan constitution does not contain a clause, found in some constitutions, making treaties, in the words of the United States Constitution, 'the supreme law of the land'. On the contrary, Article 175 provides, *inter alia*, that treaties in conflict with the constitution 'have no value whatsoever', thus giving binding effect to the international human rights instruments named in Article 46. This represents an extraordinary commitment to what has come to be called the 'international bill of rights'. Second, the inclusion within the chapter called 'Individual Rights' of the various named instruments suggests that the intention is to make them fully self-executing and available to individuals as a source of enforceable rights. Third, there is perhaps nothing surprising about a reaffirmation of the letter and spirit of the Universal Declaration and the two Covenants, which are products of the multi-ideological United Nations system. But Article 46 also refers specifically to the American Declaration of the Rights and Duties of Man and the American Convention on Human Rights, two documents entirely devoid of socialist — not to mention Marxist-Leninist — influence.

Why, then, was it necessary to spell out in elaborate detail, chapter by chapter, article by article, paragraph by paragraph, virtually every provision of the documents named in Article 46 and some additional ones to boot? They are all there: the right to life, liberty and security; to privacy; equality before the law; freedom of conscience and speech, of movement and residence; the presumption of innocence and other guarantees of due process; freedom of association; the right of petition; protection of minors and the disabled; the right to work and to strike, to food, shelter, health and much, much more.

Constitutional lawyers and theorists may relish the problems which may arise from the unusual co-existence, in a single constitution, of many detailed human rights provisions with a broad incorporation by reference of several equally long and detailed international human rights instruments. In the case of conflict between a national and an international provision, which will prevail? If a right is guaranteed internationally, but not spelled out in the national provisions, will it be enforced? What effect will the general principles of the international documents have on human rights practice in Nicaragua, such as the the statement in the Preamble of the American Declaration of the Rights and Duties of Man that 'spiritual development is the supreme end of human existence'?

There are no immediate answers. Meanwhile, it is not difficult to discern the reason for the coexistence of the long list and the short articles on human rights. After a century of authoritarian rule, followed by three decades of one of the most brutal dictatorships of this century, the Nicaraguans did not wish to leave the formulation of the gains of their revolution to a set of texts formulated by outsiders. While, as Tomás Borge has been known to say, the Sandinistas did not make their revolution to please world public opinion, the sensitivity of contemporary Nicaragua to it had some effect on the extreme detail with which the human rights provisions of the constitution were elaborated. It should be noted as well that, while some version of Article 46 is found in all three drafts of the constitution, it was always one of the more controversial articles and its incorporation in the final version was not guaranteed.

Needless to say, there are many provisions in other titles of the constitution which have a bearing on human rights, including the fundamental principles enunciated in Title I, the definition of Nicaragua as a 'democratic, participatory and representative republic' in Article 7, the provisions on the mixed economy and freedom of association in Title VI (economics), the independence of the judiciary stipulated in Article 165, the various provisions dealing with the peoples of the Atlantic Coast, and the appeal to *habeas corpus* procedures laid down in Articles 187-190.

3. Specific changes

To return to the constitutional process and to give some idea of the specificity of many of the constitution's provisions, it is interesting to consider some examples of changes which occurred between the draft submitted to the National Assembly in September 1986 and the final version promulgated in January 1987.

In the preamble the memory of Augusto César Sandino was moved from first to fourth place, following 'the struggle of our native ancestors' and references to various other national heroes. Reference to God was incorporated by listing, among those in whose name the constitution was being promulgated, 'those Christians who, from their faith in God, committed themselves to participate in the struggle for the liberation of the oppressed'.

In Article 2 of the section on Fundamental Principles, the words, 'in accordance with universal, equal, direct, free and secret suffrage' were added after 'The people exercise their power directly and through their freely elected representatives.' In Article 5 'the search for peace' was substituted for 'the struggle for a just world order' as one of the principles guiding Nicaragua's international relations. Throughout references to 'indigenous people and communities of the Atlantic Coast' have been shortened to read 'communities of the Atlantic Coast.' In Article 16 a clause was added conferring Nicaraguan nationality, upon request, to non-minors born abroad to fathers or mothers 'who were originally Nicaraguan'.

At the beginning of Title IV, Article 24, the Assembly added: 'Every person has responsibilities to their family, their community and mankind. The rights of each person are limited by the rights of others, by the security of all, and by the just demands of the general welfare' (the same text as Article 32 of the American Convention on Human Rights). In Article 25, the right to one's personality and judicial capacity was added to the right to liberty and security. A clause was added to the privacy article (26) providing that 'Letters, documents and other papers illegally seized will have no effect in judicial proceedings or elsewhere.' This principle is currently under attack by the Supreme Court of the United States and has never been followed in most European countries.

Article 27 now includes a clause conferring on foreigners the same rights, with the exception of political rights, as those enjoyed by Nicaraguan citizens. A new Article 28 accords 'the protection of the State, through its diplomatic representatives' to Nicaraguans temporarily residing abroad. The right to free expression of thought in Article 30 has been amplified by the words, 'in public or in private, individually or collectively, in oral or written or any other form'.

The following provisions were added to Article 33, dealing with detention and imprisonment:

— obligation to notify the detainee's family;
— obligation to treat detainees 'with the respect due to the dignity

inherent in the human being';
— no-one to be detained after an order for his or her release has been issued;
— convicts and persons awaiting trial to be kept in separate facilities.

The first version of Article 34 already contained the privilege against self-incrimination and, going beyond the International Covenant and the American Convention, the privilege not to testify against one's spouse and one's relatives to the fourth degree of consanguinity or the second degree of affinity. To this has now been added the privilege not to testify against one's 'companion in stable union'. Article 34 was also considerably expanded in other ways. Article 36, which establishes the right to be free from torture and cruel, inhuman or degrading treatment, now contains a clause providing that 'The violation of this right shall constitute a crime and be punished by law'. No doubt reflecting the active role played by women in the forums, Article 39 now provides that women convicts shall be kept in separate prisons staffed by female guards.

There is a new article (44) which should open up a fruitful avenue for interpretation: 'Nicaraguans have the right to that personal property which guarantees them the goods necessary and essential for their integral development.'

Another article, if fully implemented, should keep bureaucrats on their toes. To the right of petition in Article 54 has been added the right of 'constructive criticism' and the right to obtain from the authorities a reply 'within terms fixed by law'.

Article 59, obliging the state to provide for the health of the citizens, now also contains an obligation on the part of citizens to accept the sanitary measures decreed by the state.

Article 68, which provides that 'The State shall avoid the submission of the communications media to foreign interests or to the monopoly of economic power of any one group', now also prohibits prior censorship.

In the chapter on the family, Article 72, on matrimony or 'stable union', now also provides that either 'may be dissolved by mutual consent or by the will of one of the parties', and Article 78, which previously obliged the State to protect 'responsible paternity' and to investigate paternity, has added maternity to paternity.

The chapter on labour rights has been augmented by a clause (Articles 82-4) on occupational health and safety, as well as (82-7) on social security in case of incapacity, old age, illness and maternity, including one (86) on the free exercise of professions. It defines the 'just work day' as the eight-hour day (82-5).

In Title V (National Defence) the controversial reference to the 'Popular Sandinista Army' has been retained, but it has been defined as 'having a national character', and must 'protect, respect and obey' the constitution (Art. 95). The right of the citizens to arm themselves to defend their sovereignty, independence and revolutionary achievements has been supplemented by their 'right and duty to fight for the defence of life, homeland, justice, peace and the integral development of the nation' (Art.92).

In the title dealing with the economy (VI), the state now guarantees not only the various forms of property — public, private, co-operative, associative and communitarian — but also their 'democratic co-existence' (Art. 103). Article 104 has been amended to provide for the freedom of economic initiative, Article 105 to make speculation and hoarding 'grave crimes against the people', and Article 110 to make clear that the duty of the state to promote the grouping of small and medium-sized agricultural producers into more efficient units means 'voluntary grouping'.

An amendment to Title VII on education and culture makes clear that the function of education is to endow citizens not only with a scientific and humanistic, but also a critical consciousness (Art. 116). Another provides specifically for academic freedom (Art. 125).

The changes to Title VIII dealing with the powers and duties of the four branches of the government leave some questions and ambiguities:

— The President no longer has the power to appoint the Mayor of Managua, but it is unclear how the post is filled.
— The Comptroller General, whose considerable powers of supervision of the administration are now defined in Chapter IV of Title VIII, is to be elected by the National Assembly from a list proposed by the president (Art. 138-8).
— On the other hand, the president now has the power to 'direct the economy of the country and to determine the economic-social policy and programme' (Art.150-13)

A very important amendment to the chapter on 'Constitutional Control' provides that 'any citizen' may file an 'appeal of unconstitutionality' against any law, decree or regulation (Art. 187).

The new Nicaraguan constitution may well have the strongest human rights provisions of any constitution enacted to date. It also builds in provisions which can make them inoperative. Articles 150-59 and 185 provide that the President may, subject to ratification by the National Assembly within 45 days (shortened from 60 days in the previous draft), declare a State of Emergency in case of war or national catastrophe, or 'when such is required by national security or economic circumstances'. A state of emergency was declared under this provision on 9 January 1987, reimposing, with minor changes, the state of emergency already in force.[1]

Non-derogable provisions

Finally, attention must be paid to Article 186 of the new constitution, which lists no less than 71 non-derogable provisions, that is, those which may not be suspended even in a state of emergency, including all those listed as non-derogable in Article 27-2 of the American Convention on Human Rights (except for a right to a name, which is not in the constitution) and many more.

The following, among others, are non-derogable. The right to life, freedom of conscience and religion; most due process guarantees, including presumption of innocence, the right to judicial personality, equality before the law, to counsel and appeal, privilege against self-incrimination; freedom from torture and degrading treatment; the right to participate in government; the right to form or join a union, the invalidity of *ex post facto* laws, the right to one's honour and reputation, the prohibition of the death penalty and prison terms exceeding 30 years, and virtually all social and economic rights.

The following provisions, on the other hand, are derogable and currently under full or partial suspension for one year from 9 January 1987: *habeas corpus*, the rights of petition, assembly, demonstration, association and political organisation, the right to strike, freedom of speech and from censorship, inviolability of the home and correspondence, freedom of movement and domicile, the right not to be arrested except on a judicial warrant, and to a prompt trial. Curiously, one of the non-derogable articles is 46, which would seem to exempt from suspension, under international law, several of the provisions which are suspended under national law.

Prospects for the future

In an interview in November 1986 Mauricio Díaz, leader of the Popular Social Christian Party, said: 'The reservation we have about this constitution is whether or not it's ever going to take effect.'[2] In a sense, that is what everyone is waiting to see. In another sense, the judgment is too harsh.

As a contribution to the literature of human rights, the Nicaraguan constitution is already something of a landmark, with its embellishments on the standard clauses, its specific incorporation of the international law of human rights, its repeated acknowledgment of the demands of women, its novel solution to the problem of ethnic minorities, its unique mix of Latin American, social-democratic and neo-radical traditions. It will be — indeed it is already being — studied by drafters of other constitutions.

Similarly, the process by which the Nicaraguan constitution was forged will stand as an example of pluralism within revolutionary leadership. The serious and relatively low-keyed debate in the National Assembly which followed the earlier phases of party political acrimony has also made a positive contribution to the tone of political dialogue in Nicaragua, at least with those political sectors willing to engage in dialogue with the Sandinista government.

Beyond all that, over the horizon, there is the tantalising vision of a Nicaragua free from the attacks of the contras and the enmity and plotting of the US government, resisting the temptation to invoke emergency powers, giving full sway to the whole range of constitutionally guaranteed rights and becoming the first country in Latin America to have a constitution organically connected to the life and aspirations of the people.

Conclusion

Commentators have speculated to the point of tedium on possible divisions within the FSLN, especially within its nine-member directorate. The starting point of such speculations is the real division of the FSLN between 1975 and 1979 into three factions or 'tendencies'. After nearly eight years in government, however, the National Directorate's experience of unity is twice as long as that of division. There are no authoritative accounts of divisions among the nine, and this is not for want of trying to find out by diplomats, journalists and political enemies. This is not to say that there are no disagreements among the members. According to sources close to the government, disagreements do exist but they do not become stable divisions by which some could be classified as 'moderates' and others as 'hard-liners'. The fact that disagreements have not been ventilated in public is in itself an extraordinary political phenomenon.

What does this mean for human rights? Simply, that the government's record on human rights since 1979 is a better guide to its human rights policies than alleged intentions derived from study of the FSLN's grounding in Marxism-Leninism or its supposed division into 'hard-liners' and 'moderates'. It is the record of a government which has had to learn from experience, which has received advice from all quarters and often, following its own counsels, has rejected that advice. It is the record of a government which, since 1981, the Reagan administration has sought to destabilise by economic and financial blockade and war waged by a proxy army of contras.

The record we have described is not the record of a government bent on totalitarian rule. Few gross abuses can be attributed to the armed forces and the state security service, even though they have not been subject to any external regulation and citizens have not had any statutory means of seeking redress for injustices committed by them. On the contrary, there has been increasing willingness to put on trial and punish members of the armed forces accused of abuses of power. Rulings on *habeas corpus* by the Supreme Court, including the limited form permitted for security-related offences under the state of emergency, are now obeyed by the security service.

The war is enormously costly in human and material terms. The balance, however, is not completely negative. The war has forced the government to evaluate all its policies in terms of the political support they generate and to acknowledge that some of its early policies were undermining its bases of political support. This has led to sweeping changes on the Atlantic Coast and in the agrarian reform programme towards greater autonomy and independence. The same effects are felt in the field of human rights. Every wrongful arrest and false accusation undermines support for the government. The CNPPDH and the Human Rights Commission of the National Assembly are widening their roles. The government has moved to reduce time spent in pre-trial detention and to curb abusive behaviour in the interrogation phase of detention. Serving army officers and security officials have received exemplary punishment for violating human rights. There has been no repetition of the grave abuses that were committed on the Atlantic Coast in 1981 and 1982. All these improvements have taken place under a government which, from the beginning, was committed to tempering justice with mercy, through the abolition of the death penalty and, subsequently, through the policy of amnesty for the contras.

The new constitution establishes internationally recognised human and civil rights as part of Nicaraguan law. There will be enormous pressure domestically and from abroad to implement the suspended provisions of the constitution as soon as the war is clearly over. Full implementation of the constitution with all the human rights which it guarantees, however, will take many years, and will depend on Nicaragua's realising its early hopes of health, education and welfare for all. The ending of the war is an essential precondition of implementation of the constitution and this depends, now as always, on the US government.

References

CHAPTER 1: INTRODUCTION

1. José Zalaquett, *The Human Rights Issue and the Human Rights Movement*, World Council of Churches, Commission of the Churches on International Affairs, Geneva, 1981, p.7.
2. For a full discussion of this issue see Henry Shue, *Basic Rights: Subsistence, Affluence, and US Foreign Policy*, Princeton University Press, Princeton NJ, 1980.
3. Inter-American Commission on Human Rights, *Report on the situation of human rights in the Republic of Nicaragua*, Washington DC, 1981, p.151.
4. Alfonso Robelo is a millionaire industrialist who was a member of 'Los Doce' (The Twelve) — a group of prominent citizens formed in 1978 to win international support for the Sandinistas — and a non-Sandinista member of the first five-person governing *junta*. He resigned in April 1980 because of the enlargement of the Council of State from 33 to 51 members. Arturo Cruz, a senior official of the Inter-American Development Bank before 1979, was also a member of 'The Twelve'. He was President of the Central Bank of Nicaragua from July 1979 to May 1980, a member of the *junta* from May 1980 to March 1981 and ambassador to the United States from June to December 1981.
5. *Inforpress*, No.702, 14 August 1986
6. Col. John Waghelstein, 'Post-Vietnam Counterinsurgency Doctrine', *Military Review*, January 1985, p.42, cited in Sara Miles, 'The Real War: Low Intensity Conflict in Central America', *NACLA*, Vol XX, No.2, April/May 1986, p.19.
7. The following is a list of the international human rights covenants signed by Nicaragua since 1979.
   1. International Covenant on Civil and Political Rights.
   2. International Covenant on Economic, Social and Cultural Rights.
   3. American Convention on Human Rights.
   4. International Convention on the Suppression and Punishment of the Crime of Apartheid.
   5. Convention Relating to the Status of Refugees.
   6. Convention against Discrimination in Education.
   7. Convention on the Elimination of All Forms of Discrimination against Women.
   8. Declaration on Protection from Torture.
   9. Convention on the Prevention and Punishment of the Crime of Genocide.
   Nicaragua has also signed 58 of the 162 International Labour Office conventions. (The UK has signed 79, the USA 7.)
8. See 'The politics of human rights reporting', *Envío*, Vol.5, No.60, June 1986 and 'Discussion and analysis of the Americas Watch report, "Human Rights in Nicaragua, 1985-1986"', CNPPDH, *Boletin*, No.7, April-May-June 1986.

9. In a celebrated speech made on 21 February 1985, President Reagan demanded that the Sandinistas 'say uncle', an American playground expression meaning 'Give in!', by inviting the contras to participate in the government.

CHAPTER 2; THE CENTRAL AMERICAN CONTEXT

1. 'The Crisis in Central America: its origins, scope and consequences', *CEPAL Review*, No 22, April 1984, p.54.
2. Edelberto Torres-Rivas, 'Central America Today', in Martin Diskin ed. *Trouble in our Backyard*, Pantheon Books, New York, 1984, p.14.
3. Professor Tom Farer, 'Political Development in Central America: Democracy and Humanitarian Diplomacy' — Testimony presented to the National Bipartisan Commission on Central America, Washington D.C., mimeo, September 1983, p.22.
4. Roger Plant, *Guatemala: Unnatural Disaster*, Latin America Bureau, London, 1978, p.77.
5. George Black, 'Garrison Guatemala', *NACLA*, Vol XVII, No 1, Jan/Feb 1981, pp.16-17.
6. Fletcher, Lehman B. et al, *Guatemala's Economic Development: The Role of Agriculture*, Iowa State University Press, Ames, 1970, pp.25-26.
7. Alastair White, *El Salvador*, Ernest Benn, London, 1973, p.158.
8. James Dunkerley, *The Long War: Dictatorship and Revolution in El Salvador*, Junction Books, London, 1982, p.62.
9. Ibid., p.62-63.
10. Tom Barry, Beth Wood, Deb Preusch, *Dollars and Dictators*, Zed Press, London, 1982, pp. 66 & 182.
11. Latin America Bureau, *Honduras: State for Sale*, London, 1985, p.64.
12. John A. Booth, *The End and the Beginning: The Nicaraguan Revolution*, Westview Press, Boulder, Colorado, 1982, p.66.
13. David Kaimowitz and Joseph R. Thome, 'Nicaragua's Agrarian Reform: the first year', in Thomas W. Walker, ed. *Nicaragua in Revolution*, Praeger, New York, 1982, pp.224-5.
14. *CEPAL Review*, No 22, op. cit., p.62.
15. Foreign Area Studies, The American University, *Nicaragua, a country study*, Department of the Army, Washington D.C., 1982, p.115.
16. Dennis Gilbert, 'The Bourgeoisie' in Thomas W. Walker ed., *Nicaragua: The First Five Years*, Praeger, New York, 1985, p.163. Gilbert's figures are taken from the Inter-American Development Fund Report, *Social and Economic Progress in Latin America*, Washington D.C. 1978, pp. 141 & 333.
17. *CEPAL Review*, No. 22, op.cit., p.6.
18. Francisco Gamboa, quoted in J. Edward Taylor, 'Peripheral capitalism and rural-urban migration: a study of population movements in Costa Rica', *Latin American Perspectives*, Issues 25 & 26, Vol VII, Spring and Summer 1980, p. 88.
19. *CEPAL Review*, No 22, op. cit., p.60.
20. *Report of the National Bipartisan Commission on Central America*, Washington D.C., January 1984, p.21.
21. Americas Watch, *Settling into routine: human rights abuses in Duarte's second year*, New York, May 1986, p.2.
22. Ibid., p.3.
23. Tutela Legal, *Informe Anual*, 1986.
24. Chris Krueger and Kjell Enge, *Without Security or Development: Guatemala Militarised*, report submitted to the Washington Office on Latin America, mimeo, June 1985, p.2.
25. Americas Watch Committee, *Guatemala: News in Brief*, June and July 1986.

26. Americas Watch & British Parliamentary Human Rights Group, *Human Rights in Guatemala during President Cerezo's First Year*, February 1987, p.30.
27. Central America Briefing Service, *Honduras Update*, September 1986.
28. Americas Watch, *Human Rights in Honduras after General Alvarez*, February 1986, pp.28-29.

CHAPTER 3: NICARAGUA BEFORE 1979

1. Amnesty International, *The Republic of Nicaragua: An Amnesty International Report, including the findings of a mission to Nicaragua, 10-15 May 1976*, London, July 1977.
2. John A. Booth, *The End and the Beginning: The Nicaraguan Revolution*, Westview Press, Boulder, Colorado, 1982, p.163.
3. IAHCR, *Report on the situation of human rights in Nicaragua*, Washington D.C., November 1978.

CHAPTER 4: A COUNTRY AT WAR

1. Ministerio de Educación, *Documentos del 2° Congreso Nacional de Alfabetización*, Managua, 1981, p.95.
2. *International Herald Tribune*, 13, 14 May 1987.
3. US Congress, Arms Control and Foreign Policy Caucus, Washington DC, 18 April 1985. US Department of State, *Documents on the Nicaraguan Resistance: Leaders, Military Personnel and Program*, Special Report no. 142, Washington D.C., March 1986.
4. Central American Historical Institute (CAHI), *Update*, Washington DC, 31 Jan 86.
5. International Court of Justice, Affidavit of Edgar Chamorro, 5 Sept 1985.
6. WOLA, *Nicaragua: violations of the laws of war by both sides — First Supplement, January-March 1986*, Washington D.C., 1986, pp.22-23.
7. WOLA, *Nicaragua: the human tragedy of the war, April-June, 1986*, Washington D.C., 1986, p.17
8. *Barricada*, 4 July 1986.
9. Americas Watch, *Land Mines in El Salvador and Nicaragua: the civilian victims*, New York, December 1986, p.56.
10. *The Times*, London, 13 June 1986.
11. Witness for Peace, *What we have seen and heard in Nicaragua — on the scene reports 1986*, Syracuse, N.Y., 1986, p.7.
12. *Nicaragua Briefing*, CAIS, London, August 1986.
13. Richard J. Hillar, *Contra Human Rights Abuses against Honduran Citizens — A Preliminary Report*, Washington Office on Latin America, March 1986.
14. *Honduras Briefing*, CAIS, London, October 1986.
15. *Inforpress* No. 694, 19 June 1986.
16. Americas Watch, *Human Rights in Nicaragua, 1985-1986*, New York, March 1986, pp 111-115.
17. Americas Watch, *Human Rights in Nicaragua, 1985-1986*, p.112.
18. International Court of Justice, Communiqué No. 86/8, 27 June 1986, p.4.
19. Letter from Fr John Medcalf.
20. Amnesty International, *Letter to The Hon. George Schultz 21 Oct 1986, AI Index: AMR 43/06/86*, p.6.
21. Americas Watch, *Human Rights in Nicaragua, 1986*, February 1987, p.58.

22. *Envío*, Vol.5. No.62, August 1986.
23. Agencia Nueva Nicaragua, *Central America Information Bulletin*, No.51, 14 Jan 1987.
24. *Inforpress* No 681, 13 March 1986.
25. Data provided by MIDINRA.
26. WOLA, *Nicaragua: violations of the laws of war by both sides — first supplement*, January-March 1986, op.cit., p.37.

CHAPTER 5: STATES OF EMERGENCY

1. Amnesty International, *Report of the Amnesty International Missions to the Republic of Nicaragua — August 1979, January 1980 and August 1980*, London, 1982, p.34.
2. IACHR, *Annual Report 1982-1983*, p.131.
3. Comisión Permanente de Derechos Humanos,¿ *Donde Están ?*, Managua, July 1980.
4. Amnesty International, *Missions to the Republic of Nicaragua*, London 1982, p.40.
5. International Commission of Jurists, *Human Rights in Nicaragua: Yesterday and Today*, July 1980, p.50.
6. IAHCR, *Report on the situation of human rights in the Republic of Nicaragua*, Washington DC, p.75.
7. *Sunday Times*, London, 12 October 1986.
8. Amnesty International, *Missions to Nicaragua*, London, 1981, p. 24.
9. *Le Monde* 8 August 1980.
10. *Washington Post*, 19 July 1986.
11. Amnesty International, *Nicaragua: the human rights record*, London, 1986, p.25.
12. Americas Watch, *On human rights in Nicaragua*, New York, 1982, pp.64-65.
13. Lawyers Committee for International Human Rights, *Nicaragua: Revolutionary Justice*, New York, 1985, p.140.
14. Amnesty International, *Nicaragua: the human rights record*, p.31.
15. *Envío*, Vol 5., No.58, p.20.
16. Aryeh Neier, 'Critique of the report by the International League for Human Rights on Nicaragua' mimeo, New York, 1986, p.19.
17. Americas Watch, *Human Rights in Nicaragua 1985-1986*, New York, 1986, pp. 127-149.
18. Ibid., p.133.
19. US Department of State, *Inside the Sandinista Regime: A Special Investigator's Perspective*, Washington D.C., February 1986, pp. 38-46.
20. Americas Watch, *The Miskitos in Nicaragua*, New York, November 1984, p.42.
21. *Envío*, Vol.5, No.62, August 1986 gives 123 civilian deaths for the period January-July 1986; the CNPPDH (*Boletín*, December 1985) gives 1,062 investigated and confirmed killings of civilians by contra forces for the period 1980 to 30 June 1985.
22. Americas Watch, *Human Rights in Nicaragua 1985-1986*, New York, 1986, pp.33-35.
23. See also Stephen Kinzer, 'Ex-Inmates cite harsh Managua jail', *New York Times*, 23 August 1986.
24. Lawyers Committee for International Human Rights, *Nicaragua: Revolutionary Justice*, New York, April 1985, pp.96-102; Amnesty International Report 1984, p.181.
25. Americas Watch, *Human Rights in Nicaragua 1985-1986*, p.21.
26. *Washington Post*, 19 July 1986.
27. Americas Watch, *Human Rights in Nicaragua, 1986*, New York, February 1987, p. 149. (For a detailed discussion of rival estimates of the numbers of political prisoners held in Nicaragua, see pp. 149-159)
28. Americas Watch, *Human Rights in Nicaragua, 1986*, p.57.
29. Personal interview, 18 May 1987.
30. Lawyers Committee for International Human Rights, *Nicaragua: Revolutionary Justice*, New York, 1985, pp.50-51.

31. Ibid., p.49.
32. IACHR, Annual Report 1982-1983, p.18.
33. Americas Watch, *Human Rights in Nicaragua*, New York, April 1984, pp.23-24.
34. Author interview.
35. Americas Watch, *On human rights in Nicaragua*, New York, May 1982, p.32.
36. Compañera Procuradora Auxiliar Penal, Expediente No. 193, Tribunales Populares Antisomocistas.
37. Personal interview.
38. Lawyers Committee for International Human Rights, p.62. See pp.60-82 for a detailed discussion of TPA procedures.
39. Author interview with defence lawyer.
40. *Daily Telegraph*, London, 6 October 1986.
41. IACHR, *Report on the situation of human rights in the Republic of Nicaragua*, Washington D.C., June 1981, p.99.
42. Americas Watch, *On Human Rights in Nicaragua*, New York, May 1982, pp.23-24.
43. IACHR, *Report* 1981, p.26.
44. Americas Watch, *Human Rights in Nicaragua 1985-1986*, New York, 1986, p.40.
45. CAHI, *Update*, Vol.5, No.31, 24 July 1986.
46. *Barricada Internacional*, Vol.VI, No.222, 2 October 1986.
47. Bernard McCabe, quoted in CAHI, *Update*, op.cit. p.3.
48. International Committee of the Red Cross, *Central America Emergency Appeal No. 3 for 1986*, Geneva, January 1986, pp.47,48 & 62.
49. Americas Watch, *Human Rights in Nicaragua 1985-1986*, op.cit. p.42.
50. Data supplied by MIDINRA, Region VI, January 1986.
51. 'Peasant Resettlements: Protection or Pacification', *Envío*, Vol.4, Issue 48, June 1985, p.4b.
52. Americas Watch, *Human Rights in Nicaragua 1985-1986*, New York, March 1986, pp.72-74.
53. *Envío*, Vol.4, Issue 48, *op.cit.*; Tony Equale, 'The New Nicaraguan Settlements', mimeo, AFSC, Philadelphia, August 1985.
54. Equale, 'The New Nicaraguan settlements', p.10.
55. Equale, p.10.
56. Source: MIDINRA, Region VI.
57. Americas Watch, *Human Rights in Nicaragua 1985-1986*, New York, March 1986.
58. *Washington Post*, 16 July 1986.
59. Quoted in letter from Nicaragua.
60. Interview with Sebastián Castillo, secretary, *Comisión Jurídica y de Derechos Humanos*, CEPAD, 9 July 1986.
61. Interview with Dr Gustavo Parajón, President of CEPAD, *Nicaragua Update*, published by Northern California Ecumenical Council, San Francisco, Volume 7, No.3, May/June 1986.

CHAPTER 6: BASIC ECONOMIC AND SOCIAL RIGHTS

1. E.V.K. Fitzgerald, *Stabilisation and Economic Justice: the case of Nicaragua*, The Helen Kellogg Institute for International Studies, Notre Dame, Working Paper No. 34, September 1984, p.13.
2. Leonard Altilia S.J., *Education in the new Nicaragua: a preliminary report*, CAPA, Toronto, 1985, p.13.
3. Garfield, Richard and Halperin, David, 'Developments in health care in Nicaragua', *New England Journal of Medicine*, 5 August 1982.
4. CIERA, *Informe al FAO*, Managua, 1983, p.4.

5. CIERA, *Informe al FAO*, Managua, 1983, p.62.
6. 'The right of the poor to defend their unique revolution', *Envío*, No.34, July 1984.
7. *Inforpress*, No.675, 30 January 1986.
8. *Inforpress*, No.723, 22 January 1987.
9. E.V.K. Fitzgerald, *Stabilisation and Economic Justice*, p.12.
10. *Inforpress*, No.700, 31 July 1986.

CHAPTER 7: CIVIL LIBERTIES

1. Bernard Diederich, *Somoza*, Junction Books, London, 1982, pp.157-8.
2. John Spicer Nichols, 'The Media', in Thomas W. Walker, ed., *Nicaragua: The First Five Years*, Praeger, New York, 1985, pp. 183-185.
3. Liza Abelow, 'Freedom of Expression' mimeo, 1985, p.20.
4. Abelow, 'Freedom of Expression' mimeo, 1985, p.13.
5. Nick Caistor, 'A day with *La Prensa*', *Index on Censorship*, 5/86, pp. 7-8.
6. Americas Watch, *Freedom of Expression and Assembly in Nicaragua during the Election Period*, New York, December 1984, p.6.
7. Americas Watch, *Human Rights in Nicaragua, 1985-1986*, New York, March 1986, p.47.
8. Americas Watch, *Human Rights in Nicaragua*, p.47.
9. Instituto Histórico Centroamericano, 'La Prensa: post-mortem on a suicide', *Envío*, Vol.5, No. 5, pp.40-43.
10. Caistor, 'A day with *La Prensa*', p.7.
11 *Washington Post*, 3 April 1986.
12. *Inforpress*, No.696, 3 July 1986.
13. Americas Watch, *Freedom of Expression* op.cit., p.6.
14. Col. John Waghelstein, 'Post-Vietnam Counterinsurgency Doctrine', *Military Review*, January 1985, p.42, cited in Sara Miles, 'The Real War: Low Intensity Conflict in Central America', *NACLA*, Vol.XX No.2, April/May 1986, p.19.
15. *El Nuevo Diario*, 8 July 1986.
16. Americas Watch, *Human Rights in Nicaragua*, New York, May 1982, pp. 38-45.
17. *Envío*, Vol.5, No.62, p.37.
18. Abelow, p.16.
19. CAHI, *Update*, Vol.5, No.29, 17 July 1986.
20. *Washington Post*, 12 May 1986.
21. *Barricada*, 1 Sept 1986.
22. CAHI, *Update*, Vol.4, No.4., 5 Nov 1985.
23. For all these incidents, see IHCA, 'The Catholic Church and the Nicaraguan Revolution: A Chronology', *Envío*, Year 3, No.30, December 1983, pp.15b, 19b, 22b.
24. *Barricada*, 3 July 1986.
25. *Comité Evangélico Pro-Ayuda al Desarrollo*, a Protestant development organisation representing the majority of the Protestant churches in Nicaragua.
26. NCCC, Division of Overseas Ministries, *Report of a delegation to investigate 'religious persecution' in Nicaragua*, New York, mimeo, September 1984, p.4.
27. Teófilo Cabestrero, *Dieron la vida por su pueblo*, El Tayacán, Managua, 1984.
28. 'A Chain without a Cross', letter from Siuna, mimeo, 1986.
29. Witness for Peace, *What we have seen and heard in Nicaragua: on the scene reports 1986*, Syracuse, N.Y., October 1986, p.4.
30. Penny Lernoux, 'Polarisation, confusion ravage Nicaragua', *National Catholic Reporter*, 16 May 1986.
31. NCCC-USA, *Report of a delegation to investigate religious persecution in Nicaragua*, op.cit. p.20.

32. *Inforpress*, No.727, 19 February 1987.
33. *Envío*, Año 3, No.35, May 1984, p.3c.
34. ILO, *241st Report of the Committee on Freedom of Association*, Vol LXVIII, 1985, pp.186-199.
35. ILO, *233rd Report of the Committee on Freedom of Association*, Vol LXVII, 1984, p.99.
36. 233rd Report, p.199.
37. ILO, Committee on Freedom of Association, 241st Report, pp.149-54.
38. *Inforpress*, No.725, 5 February 1987.
39. Author interview, 23 Oct 1986.
40. CAHI, *Update*, Vol.5, No.29, 17 July 1986.

CHAPTER 8: THE ATLANTIC COAST

1. CIDCA, *Demografía Costeña*, Managua, July 1982, p.49.
2. Margaret D. Wilde, *The East Coast of Nicaragua: Issues for Dialogue*, report prepared for the Board of World Mission of the Moravian Church in America, June 1984, p.2.
3. CIDCA, *Trabil Nani*, Managua, 1984, p.28.
4. Klaudine Ohland and Robin Schneider, eds., *National Revolution and Indigenous Identity*, IWGIA, Copenhagen, 1983, p.1.
5. CIDCA, *Trabil Nani*, p.30.
6. Ohland and Schneider, *National Revolution*, p.16.
7. CIDCA, pp.31-32.
8. Ohland and Schneider, p.19.
9. Ohland and Schneider, p.23.
10. Americas Watch, *The Miskitos in Nicaragua, 1981-1984*, New York, 1984, p.7.
11. *Trabil Nani*, p.76.
12. *Trabil Nani*, p.67.
13. *Trabil Nani*, p.66.
14. *The Miskitos in Nicaragua, 1981-1984*, p.31.
15. Ibid.
16. Amnesty International, *Nicaragua: the human rights record*, London, 1986, p.31.
17. This account of the most recent developments on the Atlantic Coast is based on the following sources: Americas Watch, *With the Miskitos in Honduras*, New York, 11 April 1986; *CAHI*, Vol 5, Nos. 24 & 32, 19 June & 15 August 1986; *Inforpress*, Nos. 708 & 709, 25 September and 2 October 1986; *Envío*, Vol.4, No.52, October 1985 and Vol.5, No.59, May 1986.
18. *Envío*, October 1985, p.8c.
19. *Principles and Policies for the Exercise of the Right to Autonomy by the Indigenous peoples and communities of the Atlantic Coast of Nicaragua*, Managua, 1985, Section II, para 6.
20. *Principles and Policies*, Section II, para 9.
21. Americas Watch, *With the Miskitos in Honduras*, op.cit., p.20.
22. *With the Miskitos in Honduras*, p.2.
23. Comisión de Autonomía de Zelaya Sur, *Anteproyecto de Estatuto de Autonomía*, Title VI, Chapter 5, Article 48, p.18.
24. Comisión de Autonomía de Zelaya Sur, *Anteproyecto*, Title V, Art. 31, p.9.
25. According to Americas Watch, during 1986 1,700 Miskitos returned to Nicaragua under the auspices of an official UNHCR programme. The UNHCR estimates that a further 3,500-4,000 Miskitos of those who fled to Honduras in April 1986 in the KISAN-induced exodus returned directly to Nicaragua in 1986.

CHAPTER 9: THE NEW CONSTITUTION

1. States of siege and emergency are a common and perennial problem with Latin American constitutions. Indeed, Article 27 of the American Convention on Human Rights provides that 'In time of war, public danger or other emergency that threatens the independence of a State Party, it may take measures derogating from its obligations under the present Convention.' Virtually every Latin American constitution contains a similar provision and, as is all too well-known, these provisions are frequently invoked.
2. *Envío*, Vol. 5, No. 65, p.37.

Index

Note: Parties, organisations etc. which have commonly used acronyms are indexed under those. A key to abbreviations is on pages x to xii.